At Issue

Should Music Lyrics Be Censored for Violence and Exploitation?

Other Books in the At Issue Series:

Are Adoption Policies Fair?

Do Veterans Receive Adequate Health Care?

Foreign Oil Dependence

Guns and Crime

Has No Child Left Behind Been Good for Education?

How Does Advertising Impact Teen Behavior?

How Should the U.S. Proceed in Iraq?

National Security

Reality TV

Senior Citizens and Driving

Should Cameras Be Allowed in Courtrooms?

Should Drilling Be Permitted in the Arctic National Wildlife Refuge?

Should Governments Negotiate with Terrorists?

Should Juveniles Be Tried as Adults?

Should the Legal Drinking Age Be Lowered?

Should Parents Be Allowed to Choose the Gender of Their Children?

Should Social Networking Web Sites Be Banned?

Teen Driving

What Is the Future of the U.S. Economy?

At Issue

Should Music Lyrics Be Censored for Violence and Exploitation?

Roman Espejo, Book Editor

GREENHAVEN PRESS
A part of Gale, Cengage Learning

Detroit • New York • San Francisco • New Haven, Conn • Waterville, Maine • London

Christine Nasso, *Publisher*
Elizabeth Des Chenes, *Managing Editor*

For more information, contact:
Greenhaven Press
27500 Drake Rd.
Farmington Hills, MI 48331-3535
Or you can visit our Internet site at gale.cengage.com

Articles in Greenhaven Press anthologies are often edited for length to meet page requirements. In addition, original titles of these works are changed to clearly present the main thesis and to explicitly indicate the author's opinion. Every effort is made to ensure that Greenhaven Press accurately reflects the original intent of the authors. Every effort has been made to trace the owners of copyrighted material.

Cover photograph reproduced by permission of Brand X Pictures.

LIBRARY OF CONGRESS CATALOGING-IN-PUBLICATION DATA

Should music lyrics be censored for violence and exploitation? / Roman Espejo, book editor.
p. cm. -- (At issue)
Includes bibliographical references (p.) and index.
ISBN-13: 978-0-7377-4064-6 (hardcover)
ISBN-13: 978-0-7377-4065-3 (pbk.)
1. Rap (Music)--History and criticism--Juvenile literature. 2. Rap (Music)--Censorship --Juvenile literature. 3. Music--Moral and ethical aspects. 4. Censorship-- United States. I. Espejo, Roman, 1977-
ML3531.S56 2008
303.3'76--dc22

2007050857

Printed in the United States of America
1 2 3 4 5 12 11 10 09 08

ED260

Contents

Introduction

Today, hip-hop and rap music is a $4 billion-a-year industry. Not only do hip-hop and rap singles and albums dominate the Billboard music charts, the richest "hiphopreneurs" are chief executive officers of their own multimillion-dollar companies, and lucrative partnerships and contracts between such artists and international corporations have become commonplace. For instance, in 2004 rapper 50 Cent released his own beverage with Vitamin Water, which was acquired by Coca-Cola. Two years later, rapper Jay-Z sold his line of clothing, Rocawear, for $204 million to the Iconix Brand Group, which owns clothing labels such as London Fog and Mossimo. Clearly, these deals are street smart and make business sense. In recent years, the mere mention of numerous products in hip-hop and rap lyrics, such as the General Motors Cadillac Escalade and the French cognac Courvoisier, has generated millions of dollars of sales.

Far from its underground, inner-city beginnings in the 1970s, hip-hop and rap music has also received increased recognition for artistic merit from America's most venerated establishments in music and entertainment. The Grammy Awards, which is sponsored by the National Academy of Recording Arts and Sciences, established the Grammy Award for Best Rap Album in 1996, sixteen years after the Sugar Hill Gang's "Rapper's Delight" became the first hip-hop single to break into the Top 40. In addition, rapper Eminem won the 2003 Academy Award for Best Original Song for "Lose Yourself," which Eminem wrote for the loosely autobiographical role he played in the motion picture *8 Mile.* It was the first hip-hop single to earn such an achievement. Three years later, to stunned and mixed reactions, hip-hop group Three 6 Mafia won the 2006 Academy Award for Best Original Song for "It's

Hard Out Here for a Pimp," featured in the motion picture *Hustle & Flow*, defeating the critically acclaimed rock band U2.

Eminem's and Three 6 Mafia's wins at the Academy Awards have not gone without fervent criticism. Critics especially decried the Academy's decision to choose "It's Hard Out Here for a Pimp" as its Oscar winner. African American musician Joaquin Jessup states that "it was another example of how they pick the worst aspects of black life and reward that." Expressing his concern for how African Americans are portrayed in the media, Jessup also argues that "the only place many people see our culture is through movies and on television, and at the same time, this country is experiencing an influx of people coming over here from all over the world, and the only thing they see of black America through the media is . . . pimps and gangsters and all of that. It's always some low-down brother or some welfare mother."

Other critics, however, are more troubled by what they view as a hypocritical relationship between white, corporate America and black artists: While the white-dominated media criticize hip-hop and rap lyrics for being misogynistic, violent, and materialistic, white-owned corporations—such as record companies and apparel manufacturers—profit from the sales of violent, exploitative hip-hop and rap music or rappers' product endorsements. National Action Network president Al Sharpton, for example, aims "to create an environment where the myriad of companies that benefit from the success of hip-hop feel a true sense of responsibility to the young Americans who love and support the music." He contends that the recording industry takes "responsibility for the ultimate reality shows they have created," when the rivalries of rappers explode into violence, by penalizing them. According to Sharpton, "Orchestrated makeup sessions and giving checks to charity are simply not enough to make up for the culture of violence and the mind-set that this type of behavior foists on our communities."

The viewpoints of Joaquin Jessup and Al Sharpton embody the complex issues surrounding the censorship, labeling, and restriction of popular music. The violence and exploitation in music lyrics are at the center of several debates: the freedom of speech; the effect of violent and sexual imagery on children; sexism and racism in the media, entertainment, and culture; and the responsibilities of recording artists and the companies that support them. In *At Issue: Should Music Be Censored for Violence and Exploitation?*, authors and experts from diverse professional, political, and personal backgrounds investigate one of popular music's main controversies.

1

Lyrics with Violence and Exploitation Harm Young People

Lloyd Eby

Lloyd Eby is assistant senior editor in the Currents in Modern Thought section of the World & I, *a monthly educational magazine.*

Instead of literature, art, and other traditions, popular music—especially rock and rap music—plays the most influential role in youth culture. Much of this music is controversial; numerous popular rock and rap artists explore troubling social issues and themes of violence, sexuality, and alienation. The most talented use creativity, depth, and irony in their lyrics. The youngest consumers of this music, however, are at risk of psychological harm because they are unable to recognize or comprehend these artistic complexities and take song lyrics at face value. To them, the words of rock and rap artists are instructional, imparting not only vernacular and other habits of speech, but apathetic and unhealthy views on violence, sexual behavior, gender, and society.

The best discussion I have seen of the role and influence of music in the lives of today's young people occurs in the "Music" chapter of the late Allan Bloom's 1997 book, *The Closing of the American Mind.* Bloom had been a professor of social thought at the University of Chicago and other universities for many years, and he drew on his experiences interacting with and teaching numerous generations of students.

Lloyd Eby, "Why Eminem Is a Problem," *World & I Online (WorldAndIJournal.com)*, March 2003. Reproduced by permission.

Bloom begins by noting that today's students do not have books, but they do have music: "Nothing is more singular about this generation than its addiction to music. This is the age of music and the states of soul that accompany it." Moreover, advances in technology have made music available to all people, everywhere, all the time. "The musical soil has become tropically rich," Bloom says, and "there are many geniuses, producing all the time," so that "there is no dearth of the new and the startling."

"Young people know that rock [music] has the beat of sexual intercourse."

A change in the role of music in young people's lives came about recently, Bloom says—he seems to mean at the beginning of the 1960s. Before that there had been a decline in the role and influence of music; romanticism had dominated serious music since Beethoven, he says, and this appealed to refined sentiments that barely exist in the contemporary world. Moreover, there had been a divide between the middle and lower classes, the educated and the uneducated. The educated middle class frequently "made some of the old European music a part of the home, partly because they liked it, partly because they thought it was good for the kids." But rock music, when it emerged, came with "real, if coarse, feelings as opposed to artificial and dead ones." This amounted to a revolution, and rock music "won the revolution and reigns unabashed today." The class distinction in musical tastes disappeared because rock appealed to all young people, regardless of class or education. "The power of music in the soul . . . has been recovered after a long period of desuetude [disuse]. And it is rock music that has effected this restoration." . . .

A Barbaric Appeal

Rock music, Bloom says, seeks and serves to unleash the Dionysian [frenzied] passions, to "replenish our dried-up stream from barbaric sources." Rock music "has risen to its current heights in the education of the young on the ashes of classical music, and in an atmosphere in which there is no intellectual resistance to tap the rawest passions." It has "one appeal only, a barbaric appeal, to sexual desire—not love, . . . but sexual desire undeveloped and untutored." It "acknowledges the first emanations of children's emerging sensuality and addresses them seriously, eliciting them and legitimating them . . . as the real thing." It and the entertainment industry "give children, on a silver platter, . . . everything their parents always used to tell them they had to wait for until they grew up and would understand better." That thing is sex. "Young people know that rock [music] has the beat of sexual intercourse."

The result of this sexual interest that is expressed in rock music is "rebellion against the parental authority that represses it." The selfishness of teenagers "becomes indignation and then transforms itself into morality." Along with this came the sexual revolution, which overthrew "the forces of domination, the enemies of nature and happiness." This led to a transformation in which "a worldview is balanced on the sexual fulcrum." Moreover, these changes had harmful consequences because "nothing noble, sublime, profound, delicate, tasteful or even decent can find a place in such tableaux. There is room only for the intense, changing, crude and immediate." This leads to pubescent children whose bodies "throb with orgasmic rhythms," and whose "life is made into a nonstop commercially packaged [sexual] fantasy." He goes on to say that his description "may seem exaggerated, but only because some would prefer to regard it as such."

All this takes place in a "family spiritual void [that] has left the field open to rock music"; parents "cannot possibly forbid their children to listen to it" since it is everywhere and "all children listen to it." Because of that, "forbidding it would simply cause [parents] to lose their children's affection and obedience." The result is "nothing less than parents' loss of control over their children's moral education at a time when no one else is seriously concerned with it."

The rock music business fully supports all this because it is "perfect capitalism, supplying to demand and helping to create it." It is a business that "is peculiar only in that it caters almost exclusively to children, treating legally and naturally imperfect human beings as though they were ready to enjoy the final or complete satisfaction." It leads to a "loss of a clear view of what adulthood or maturity is, and our incapacity to conceive ends." Because it is empty of values, it leads to "the acceptance of the natural facts as the ends." The end, in the case of rock music, is "infantile sexuality," and, Bloom suspects, because of the absence of other, better ends, many adults have come to agree with those ends.

Bloom's ultimate concern is "not with the moral effects of this music—whether it leads to sex, violence or drugs." Instead, he is concerned about education and the fact that because the young people are addicted to the music, they cannot discover the depths of thought and experience that lie within great books, art, and the great traditions. "As long as they have the Walkman [portable music player] on," he concludes, "they cannot hear what the great tradition has to say. And, after the prolonged use, when they take it off, they find they are deaf." He means not that they are physically deaf, but that their minds and spirits have become seared, so they are unable to comprehend.

The precognitive, emotive force of music and lyrics can influence people for good or ill.

An important point that Bloom ignores is that the precognitive, emotive force of music and lyrics can influence people for good or ill. Bloom focuses on the bad effects of rock music on the young, and he is surely correct that much of this influence is bad. But some music also affects young people who hear it in good and beneficial ways. Examples are nursery songs, religious and patriotic music, and even some forms of rock music or rock songs—so-called Christian or religious rock attempts to do this.

The PMRC and Tipper Gore

In 1984, Tipper Gore, wife of then-senator Albert Gore, bought the album *Purple Rain* by the artist then known as Prince. When listening to the album with her daughter, Gore became very disturbed by some of the lyrics, especially the song "Darling Nikki," about a woman caught masturbating in a hotel with a magazine. This outraged Gore, and she started wondering whether other parents who had bought this album for their children had also listened to it and become upset at its contents. After studying other song lyrics, music videos, and the MTV music network, she became increasingly agitated. Eventually, she published a best-selling book on the topic, *Raising a PG Kid in an X-rated Society* (1987).

Gore joined with some other influential Washington wives in forming the Parents' Music Resource Center (PMRC). The stated goal of the PMRC was not to push for government censorship of the recording industry—a claim made by the group's opponents—but instead to "educate and inform parents about this alarming new trend as well as to ask the industry to exercise self-restraint." On September 19, 1985, representing the PMRC, Tipper Gore and Susan Baker, wife of Treasury Secretary James Baker, appeared before the Senate Committee on Commerce, Science and Transportation. [Susan] Baker, speaking to the committee, said:

"Our primary purpose is to educate and inform parents about this alarming trend as well as to ask the industry to exercise self-restraint. . . .

"Because anything that we are exposed to that much [as today's rock music] has some influence on us, we believe that the music industry has a special responsibility, as the message of songs goes from the suggestive to the blatantly explicit.

"As [journalist] Ellen Goodman stated in a recent column . . . 'The outrageous edge of rock and roll has shifted its focus from Elvis's pelvis to the saw protruding from Blackie Lawless's codpiece on a WASP album. Rock lyrics had turned from "I can't get no satisfaction" to "I am going to force you at gunpoint to eat me alive."

"The material we are concerned about cannot be compared with 'Louie Louie,' Cole Porter, Billie Holiday, etc. Cole Porter's 'the birds do it, the bees do it,' can hardly be compared with WASP, 'I f--- like a beast.' There is a new element of vulgarity and violence toward women that is unprecedented." . . .

The PMRC members stressed that they wanted four things: (a) that questionable lyrics should be printed and provided with their respective recordings; (b) that objectionable album covers should be sold in plain brown wrappers, or sold in areas segregated from other albums; (c) that rock concerts be rated; and (d) that MTV segregate questionable video recordings into specific late-night viewing slots. In addition, the PMRC claimed that "virgin minds" were being poisoned by "hidden messages and backward masking." Besides its testimony before Congress, the PMRC lobbied recording companies to reassess the contracts of performers whose works were found to be objectionable.

The PMRC never called for direct government censorship of music lyrics; in fact, its members explicitly denied that they were advocating censorship. They stated repeatedly that they were working toward adoption of a "voluntary" ratings system. But the testimony and proposals of the PMRC stirred up a hornets' nest within the music industry and among some prominent musicians, Frank Zappa being the most notable. He too testified before that Senate committee, speaking strongly against the PMRC and its proposals, saying that "censorship here would be like using decapitation to deal with dandruff." He argued that any ratings system "opens the door to an endless parade of moral quality-control programs based on Things Certain Christians Don't Like. What if the next bunch of Washington Wives demands a large yellow 'J' on material written or performed by Jews?" Musical performers who were antiratings formed a group called Musical Majority, affiliated with the American Civil Liberties Union, and with some record companies.

In the 1990s, Tipper Gore became more or less silent on these issues and quit as head of the PMRC. By that time, others, such as Vice President Dan Quayle and [actor] Charlton Heston, had taken up the cause.

Rap Lyrics and Charlton Heston

Bloom's comments about rock music and its effects on young people apply today with even more force to rap music also known as hip-hop. As noted above, the effects of music and lyrics can be for good or ill. Here we are concerned with the ill effects, which are more prevalent and common than the good ones. Rap, like rock, had its roots in the black American underground—urban in this case—but has broken out to become a major force in the music of most young people, of whatever race or class. And it has usually been far more vulgar (using the f word over and over), explicitly sexually oriented, violence-affirming, hate-filled, and misogynistic than the worst of rock ever was.

At a Harvard University Law School forum on February 16, 1999, Heston—Academy Award–winning actor and National Rifle Association president—gave a presentation entitled "Winning the Cultural War." He mentioned President Lincoln's proclamation in the Gettysburg Address, "Now we are engaged in a great Civil War, . . ." and said, "Those words are true again. I believe that we are again engaged in a great civil war, a cultural war that is about to hijack your birthright."

In the course of his talk, Heston mentioned an incident having to do with the lyrics of rap music, stating:

> A few years back I heard about a rapper named Ice-T who was selling a CD called "Cop Killer," celebrating ambushing and murdering police officers. It was being marketed by none other than Time/Warner, the biggest entertainment conglomerate in the world. Police across the country were outraged. Rightfully so—at least one had been murdered. But Time/Warner was stonewalling because the CD was a cash cow for them, and the media were tiptoeing around because the rapper was black. I heard Time/Warner had a stockholders meeting scheduled in Beverly Hills. I owned some shares at the time, so I decided to stand. What I did there was against the advice of my family and colleagues. I asked for the floor. To a hushed room of a thousand average American stockholders, I simply read the lyrics of "Cop Killer"—every vicious, vulgar, instructional word.—I got my 12 gauge sawed off / I got my headlights turned off / I'm about to bust some shots off / I'm about to dust some cops off. . . ." It got worse, a lot worse. I won't read the rest of it to you. . . . The room was a sea of shocked, frozen, blanched faces. The Time/Warner executives squirmed in their chairs and stared at their shoes. They hated me for that. Then I delivered another volley of sick lyric brimming with racist filth, where Ice-T fantasizes about sodomizing two 12-year-old nieces of Al and Tipper Gore. "She pushed her butt against my. . . ." Well, I won't do to you here what I did to them. Let's just say I left the room in echoing silence. When I read the lyrics to the waiting press corps, one of them said, "We can't print that." "I know," I replied, "but Time/Warner's selling it." . . .

It is interesting that defenders of this music, such as Frank Zappa, almost always jump to the conclusion that critics, such as the PMRC, want to institute some form of government censorship. The critics explicitly state that their goals are different: they want such things as open labeling, parental notification, printed lyrics, and restraint on the part of artists and the music business. The problem seems to be that the defenders, in this domain at least, cannot think in categories other than individual freedom contrasted with government control, while the critics work from different concepts, thinking in terms of personal and community standards and of personal and community responsibility for upholding those standards.

People as young as six to twelve . . . are not at the level where they make cognitive assessments of irony, or any true or false claims about the content.

Marshall Mathers III, known as Eminem, has become the most prominent present-day rap or hip-hop artist. His most important work is the CD entitled *The Eminem Show*, and the movie featuring him, *8 Mile*. The greatest irony is that Eminem is white, in an industry and musical-form that have been predominately black, a state of affairs he remarks on in the song "White America":

"When I was underground, no one gave a f--- I was white, no labels wanted to sign me, almost gave up, I was like /"

"F--- it, until I met Dre, the only one to look past, gave me a chance, and I lit a fire up under his ass."

Those few lyrics encapsulate what I will call the Eminem problem. One must give due recognition to Eminem's musical and lyrical genius. He became preeminent in his field not by a fluke, but because he is among the very best musicians and lyricists of the day. His work is characterized by inventiveness, apposite and unexpected lines and line combinations, and layers of complexity. Moreover, his stance in the lyrics is frequently ironic, in that he comments on the reactions that objectors are likely to have to them. He also deals with topics that have almost never been handled in rock music: the death of his father, the devastating results of divorce, his concern for his daughter, and his desire that his mother behave well. On the other hand, his lyrics and movie pulsate with vulgarity, adolescent sexuality, hatred, misogyny, and violence:

"So now I'm catchin the flack from these activists when they raggin, actin like I'm the first rapper to smack a bitch, or say faggot/"

"shit, just look at me like I'm your closest pal, the poster-child, the motherf---in spokesman now for."

The consumers of this music—the people as young as six to twelve years old who listen to and buy it—are not at the level where they make cognitive assessments of the irony, or any true or false claims about the content. Thus, Eminem and his music, as well as his film *8 Mile* and his public persona, raise anew the problem of the relationship between artistic goodness or achievement, on the one hand, and ethical or social goodness, on the other. Although, as Bloom notes, romanticism has been eclipsed today, its stance toward art and the artist still largely holds. It can be characterized, possibly a bit oversimply, as holding that feeling is more important than reason, and, since its rise, has held sway in much of elite thought about the role and status of art and artists. Consequently, the sophisticated view or attitude has usually been to treat the art and the artist as beyond ethical assessment, as open only to consideration of whether the art is good—"good" here usually meaning avant-garde, shocking, or otherwise unconventional. If the art is good, then, according to this view, it is therefore valuable; if the artist makes good art, he is beyond good and evil.

There are, however, good reasons to suspect that this view is mistaken. We know that attraction to art or being a great artist does not necessarily make that person ethically good as a person. Two examples are Adolf Eichmann, the Nazi death camp commander, who played violin and liked violin music, and Pablo Picasso, whose work most knowledgeable art historians consider to have been one of the highest points of twentieth-century art, but who, as [columnist and author] Arianna Stassinopoulos Huffington showed in [the book] *Picasso: Creator and Destroyer*, was a misogynist and monster. . . .

Music is not an argument; it does not consist of statements that are to be understood as true or false. Instead, music operates at a precognitive level of human apprehension. So Bloom is correct in what he wrote in his account of Plato, "Music is the soul's primitive and primary speech . . . without articulate speech or reason." This observation is not made on the basis of Plato's supposed authority. Instead, Plato made it because it is true, and its truth does not depend on whether he had a comprehensive philosophy of anything. Those who object to the lyrics of rap music do not take those lyrics to be statements that could be true or false. Instead, they take them to be a form of primitive and primary speech, prereason. Such primitive speech is very much a compelling force, just as the beat of rock or the drums of Indian dancers are a compelling force. In fact, the force is such that it bypasses the reasoning part of the human mind and urges or even compels thoughts and behaviors that, on reflection, the person may repudiate.

Much of rock and especially rap music immerses young people in vile language, premature sex, gun play and other forms of violence, misogyny, and hatred.

Much of rock and especially rap music immerses young people in vile language, premature sex, gun play and other forms of violence, misogyny, and hatred. Although it depicts Eminem sympathetically and shows him struggling to rise above and escape his surroundings, the movie *8 Mile* does all of those. The movie and Eminem's lyrics do not make an argument for these things—his lyrics and the film can be understood, on the cognitive level, as questioning them or making ironic comments about them. But the cognitive level is not the one on which rap operates on six to twelve year olds. It influences them precognitively, insinuating itself into their spirits, so to speak, in such a way that their young selves are formed, without their conscious knowledge or consent, into its way of being and outlook. It is an expression of the nihilism of the day. In schools across the land, beginning as early as elementary school, one sees young people with earphones seemingly glued to their heads, bopping and swaying to the music, then talking and acting as the rappers talk and act.

One would be quite foolish to claim that there is no direct connection between young people's immersion in rock and rap music—drenched as those musics are in adolescent sex, violence, and misogyny—and the rise in actual teenage sex, with its attendant pregnancies and sexually transmitted diseases, and the increase in teenage violence, shootings, and other pathologies. This is not just simple correlation; there is surely a causal factor, too.

Someone commenting on Eminem said that the Right worries about sex and the Left about violence. I am not opposed either to sex or to guns, per se. I think that sex between married adult heterosexual couples is the place where the divine enters most directly into human life. I also own and shoot numerous rifles and shotguns, either at targets or hunting. But those are not the mature and responsible expressions of sex and guns that exist in Eminem's music; the sex in his music is adolescent, or adulterous, and mixed with misogyny, and the gunplay is stupid and violently directed at humans. Since we know that young people learn and mimic what they see and hear—to say otherwise is to deny all theories and knowledge about education—we know for certain that they are absorbing diabolical attitudes and behaviors about sex and violence from his music.

O'Reilly Understands

In his syndicated newspaper column of November 18, 2002, [political commentator] Bill O'Reilly compared Eminem to Elvis Presley: "In 1962, a young truck driver named Elvis Presley had become a rock superstar singing about hound dogs, tender love and his mama, whom he apparently loved." But Eminem "has become the country's hottest recording star rapping about rape, drugs and his mother, whom he apparently hates. She has sued him for $10 million. He called her a 'slut' in one of his recordings." O'Reilly goes on to note the profound effect Elvis had on young Americans: "Millions of young boys slicked back their hair and adopted some Elvis moves on the dance floor."

O'Reilly sees Eminem's influence as much more sinister. "Eminem has left his calling card as well. Two New York City grammar school teachers told me it is not uncommon for 10-year-old boy to call the little girls in their classes 'bitches' and 'hos' (whores)." It's true, unfortunately, that very many urban American young people as young as six years old talk this way and did so long before Eminem came on the scene. But his songs only reinforce this trend, encouraging even more youngsters to think and talk this way.

O'Reilly minces no words. "Any way you slice it, Marshall Mathers sells degenerate behavior to kids. The entertainment industry, long devoid of any social conscience whatsoever, provides Mr. Mathers with cover and calls him a creative genius and a sensitive soul. Students of history will remember that they called Caligula [the Roman Emperor considered sexually perverse and cruel] that once as well."

The problem, O'Reilly claims, is that there has been a progressive degeneration of popular culture that has left us shell-shocked, and we have "run out of outrage." "The Baby Boom generation," he says, "embraced Elvis but then went progressively off the deep end. Drugs became chic, rebellion against authority a fad, greed became good and self-indulgence ruled."

All this has "produced an army of degenerates like Eminem." We should not be surprised, he says, "when 10-year-old Timmy calls his baby sister a bitch," because "Timmy hears that word and worse all the time." Moreover, "he sees his idol Eminem being praised by adults on TV."

O'Reilly concludes, "If you think this Eminem person is harmless, you are astonishingly wrong. Like Elvis, he will leave his mark on America. But unlike Elvis, the legacy Mathers will leave is one that will injure many children, especially those without much parental guidance."

What O'Reilly writes could be attacked for lacking nuance, and he does not acknowledge the artistic or aesthetic subtlety of Eminem. But O'Reilly does understand the problem of the influence of Eminem and his music well enough on young people and their culture that his indictment of it is correct. It teaches young people styles of talking and being and attitudes about sex, other people, violence, and culture that can and will cause them great harm.

In the first days of January of the new year [2003], as this was being prepared for printing, word came through MTV—was it a serious bulletin or a spoof—that Eminem has announced that he is returning to his wife and giving up drugs. He has commented that it is time to put his past behavior behind him, because one cannot be young and behave in stupid ways all the time. Time will tell whether this is serious and whether it is carried out. But if the announcement is true and if Eminem does follow through, it will be a most important development for this complex artist.

2

Censoring and Restricting Lyrics Harms Society

Paul D. Fischer

Paul D. Fischer is an associate professor in the Department of Recording Industry at Middle Tennessee State University in Murfreesboro.

Historical and political perspectives demonstrate that music censorship and restriction in America are attempts at maintaining Eurocentric, middle-class social norms and silencing minority voices in an increasingly diverse nation. Rock and rap music continue to meet mainstream resistance, regulation, and censorship—as jazz and blues did in the previous decades—because of prominent ties to African American culture and the working class. Moreover, current laws such as the USA Patriot Act and ratings systems threaten the First Amendment rights and civil liberties of musicians who hold dissenting views on politics or dominant cultural values. Because it provokes much-needed criticisms and meaningful discussions about the issues facing the world, popular music must be protected against censorship and restriction.

In terms of historical time, the two hundred twenty-plus year history of the United States of America is an instant. In terms of governance by the rule of law, the effectiveness of the United States Constitution over a slightly shorter period is a modern marvel. In addition to setting up the workings of a

Paul D. Fischer, "What if They Gave a Culture War and Nobody Came? Prospects for Free Musical Expression in the United States," *Freemuse*, January 28, 2003. Reproduced by permission.

form of representative government, it grants numerous, substantial rights to citizens (initially property owning white males, now somewhat more egalitarian), protecting and empowering them in their encounters with State power. Fundamental among these rights are those set out in the First Amendment to the Constitution:

> Congress shall make no law respecting an establishment of religion, or prohibiting the free exercise thereof; or abridging freedom of speech, or of the press; or the right of the people to peaceably assemble and to petition the government for a redress of grievances.

With regard to freedoms of speech and the press, a landmark case with implications for popular music was settled in 1735. New York newspaperman John Peter Zenger was charged with libel by the British authorities for the content of the *New York Weekly Journal* which he published, but did not write. The case, which Zenger won, is usually discussed in terms of its significance as a departure from British libel law, and a victory for colonial press freedom. In this context, some of the allegedly libelous material must be considered at face value. Part of what Zenger published were lyrics to ballads lampooning the British colonial governor and his cronies, and he was exonerated. From this point forward, song lyrics were presumptively protected speech in America. If there is any lingering doubt, in a 1985 opinion in the case *Cinevision Corp. v. City of Burbank*, the Court of Appeals for the 9th Circuit plainly stated: "music is a form of expression that is protected by the First Amendment." Even with this protection, the security of music as expression in America is not assured and begs closer scrutiny.

Despite the Constitutional provision that Congress, the legislature, "make no law," the Supreme Court, the nation's highest judicial authority has, over the years, identified three areas of speech that fall outside the First Amendment's protection. These are obscenity, inciteful speech or "fighting words," and speech that could cause harm to minors. Popular music has been challenged in court in all these areas. Before examining these challenges and their future implications in detail, consider just a bit more cultural context. Due to its brief history as a nation, the United States has thus far defined itself more through ideals, myths, and heroes, than concrete realities achieved over centuries and millennia. Myths tell stories that flesh out the bedrock values the nation is striving to achieve, and heroes embody them. Central to the character of America is the composition of its people, often told through a history of European immigration and conquest, beginning with the Mayflower. However, to fully tell that story, Africans in the Middle Passage, Irish, Italians, eastern Europeans, Jews from all of Europe, and more recently Hispanics and Asians must be included in the mix. The American narrative that speaks to this condition is "The Myth Of the Melting Pot." At its most basic, this tale posits America as a promised land, full of wealth and opportunity for immigrants of all stripes, that anyone can become an American, work hard and prosper. There are, however, two compelling and competing readings of this myth.

An Assimilationist Model

The more orthodox reading of the myth presents an assimilationist model: all who come to America should acknowledge and accept existing power structures, societal practices, and cultural norms. In wanting to live here, the immigrant embraces America as a somehow "better" place, and in going through the hardships of immigration, adaptation to the new environment and the quest for citizenship, submits to the heat of the crucible and emerges Americanized and fit for mainstream life. This is fine for the status quo, but devalues cultures of origin, denying the immigrants' ability to contribute meaningfully to the culture of this young nation while taking pride in their culture of origin. The more progressive reading of the myth embraces that diversity, and has been around for some time. Written in 1916, [progressive writer] Randolph Bourne's essay "Trans-National America" argued that America was leading the way toward an egalitarian global consciousness that could serve humanity well in the centuries to come. He wrote:

> Only America, by reason of its unique liberty of opportunity and traditional isolation for which she seems to stand, can lead in this cosmopolitan enterprise. Only the American—and in this category I include the migratory alien who has lived with us and caught the pioneer spirit and a sense of new social vistas—has the chance to become a citizen of the world. America is coming to be, not a nationality, but a trans-nationality, a weaving back and forth with other lands, of many threads of all sizes and colors. Any movement which attempts to threaten this weaving or dye the fabric any one color, or disentangle the threads of the strands, is false to this cosmopolitan vision.

The ongoing internal tensions of defining American culture figure profoundly in discussions of our popular music.

This cosmopolitan America is emerging, despite the opposition of pro-assimilationist individuals and groups. Census data suggest that by 2010 America's population will consist of a "majority of minorities." Despite this reality on the ground, many influential Americans deny the cultural significance of this state of affairs, and continue to argue for a Caucasian dominated, European-centered, unified mainstream culture for the nation. For example, *Chicago Tribune* columnist Clarence Page saw this in the statements and actions of Supreme Court Justice Antonin Scalia:

> Like many other Americans, Scalia appears to subscribe to the "melting pot" theory, a vision in which all of America's

> races, cultures and ethnic groups are expected to stir themselves into the cultural mainstream, ipso facto, "e pluribus unum."
>
> Charming as that vision may be, it defies some obvious realities. For many Americans this nation is less a melting pot than a multi-racial, multi-ethnic mulligan stew. Everyone contributes flavors and textures to the pot without sacrificing individual group identities.

The ongoing internal tensions of defining American culture figure profoundly in discussions of our popular music. The fact that many non-European musical traditions (especially African) are integral to its evolution causes problems for the assimilationists, who, despite the American Revolution, still look to Europe for models of the pinnacles of human cultural attainment. Ethnomusicologists, however, often point to New Orleans' Congo Square as the birthplace of uniquely American music, a place where European and African traditions mingled with little commercial or political regulation. "Jass" emerged from this milieu.

Opposite From the "Others"

Another means mainstream America has used to define itself during its brief history has been to emphasize what it is not. The presence of enemies, military or otherwise, has provided opportunities to magnify the negative points perceived in those opposed to America, or "The American Way Of Life." It can then be argued that this nation stands for all that is good and opposite from the ways of those Others, a rhetorical means of creating moral high ground, seizing it, then using it as a bully pulpit. For much of the twentieth century, the Cold War and American politicians' abhorrence of Communists served this purpose. At times, zealots like Senator Joseph McCarthy of Wisconsin [who in the 1950s sought to expose Communists living in America] even looked within the nation to identify those who embodied or expressed the views of the enemy. The pattern continues. After the fall of the Berlin Wall and the collapse of the Soviet Union, the United States had no substantive external enemies. This proposed a challenge to those who felt comfortable defining this society in terms of what it wasn't. Some looked within.

Among these is Patrick Buchanan, former [president] Nixon speechwriter and Presidential candidate, who was instrumental in declaring a "culture war" in the United States with columns like "Losing The War For America's Culture" in *The Washington Times* (May 22nd, 1989). His most recent book *The Death of the West* argues that a cultural revolution has been waged and won by "cultural Marxists," saying:

> In a third of a century, what was denounced as the counterculture has become the dominant culture, and what was the dominant culture has become, in Gertrude Himmelfarb's phrase, "a dissident culture." America has become an ideological state, a "soft tyranny" where the new orthodoxy is enforced, not by police agents, but by inquisitors of the popular culture.

He decries the fact that songwriters have replaced poets in the consciousness of the young, making the likes of [Beatle] John Lennon "the poet laureate of a generation." The notion of culture war makes enemies of otherwise law-abiding Americans (and others) for their role in the creation of elements of culture. By reducing the nuanced, expressive world of cultural creation to an Us vs. Them binary, some of those in power and with access to the media have attempted to frame this discussion in strictly assimilationist terms. Fortunately, the culture itself, including elements created by people of diverse origins and influences, seems more progressive. All involved acknowledge that the ongoing definition of American culture is in play here, so the stakes are high. The struggle is likely to continue.

Among America's first European immigrants were the Puritans, who sought religious freedom. They were not, however, especially tolerant of the ways of others. This seems to be the way of the assimilationists, who often speak of the "intent of the framers" of the Constitution, in efforts to disallow more egalitarian interpretation of the nation's founding documents than would have prevailed in the 18th century. The problems they have with aspects of American culture, that they have "gone to war" against, are not so much that what they see and hear is patently un-American, but not in concert with *their* America. They seem to have an expectation of being able to set societal standards for all, from the top down, despite the precedent of the Zenger case which was known to the framers.

The Eurocentric aesthetic of mainstream popular music allowed experimentation with "exotic" flavors, but in small doses.

An Uneasy Relationship

As a nation, the United States has an uneasy relationship with its musical heritage. Despite global recognition of the originality of its musics, a product of its multicultural population, mainstream America chooses not to bask in this glory. The Eurocentric aesthetic of mainstream popular music allowed experimentation with "exotic" flavors, but in small doses. The industry did not permit them to dominate. Full acceptance of outsiders only went so far. Many of the most successful commercial songwriters of the industry's early twentieth century Tin Pan Alley phase were immigrant Jews, but the mainstream accommodated them. In the twentieth century, Jews became "white folks." Not so for the descendants of slaves, and other nonwhite minorities. Jazz, blues, ragtime, rhythm and blues, rock 'n' roll, and hip-hop draw more on African sources than European ones for their spark. This has been a trigger of mainstream resistance. Second, these musics found their way to popularity in white culture mainly through working class channels, usurping presumed elites' role in taste making. This has caused these innovative, indigenous forms to be labeled "raw," "primitive," "base," and even "the devil's music." There are sincere, patriotic mainstream Americans who believe the popularity of these musics signals the end of Western Civilization, not the apogee of America's cultural output thus far. It is this fundamental tension in American views of culture that has made popular music a frequent battlefield in the so-called "culture wars." . . .

Thus far, America's courts have provided a substantive check on the wishes of legislators to regulate speech in instances where popular music could be impacted. Another law, which could change all this, must be mentioned here, but the sweeping nature of its language and lack of a record of enforcement attempts under its provisions make discussion of it entirely speculative. This is the USA Patriot Act, "Uniting and Strengthening America by Providing Appropriate Tools Required to Intercept and Obstruct Terrorism" (Pub. L. No. 107-56) (also "USA Patriot" or "The Act"), passed in the wake of the attacks of September 11th, 2001. This law could impact politically engaged popular music and artists most drastically.

Cases Decided

As mentioned above, popular music has been challenged in court on the grounds that it has fallen into one of the three areas Supreme Court jurisprudence has left unprotected by the First Amendment, obscenity, inciteful speech (fighting words), or causing harm to minors. Government, however, is not the only source of legal action. In the obscenity case involving music, the artist initiated the action. In February of 1990 a Broward County (Florida) Sheriff purchased a copy of *As Nasty As They Wanna Be* by 2Live Crew and transcribed the lyrics of six of its eighteen tracks. He requested a finding of probable cause on obscenity, and in March, Judge Mel Grossman issued an advisory opinion that the material was probably obscene. On that advice, Sheriffs in uniform delivered letters to area record retailers "as a matter of courtesy" that further sales would result in their arrest. The next week, Skyywalker Records filed suit on the question of obscenity and whether the Sheriffs had put an illegal prior restraint on the recording. Judge Jose Gonzalez found both an illegal prior restraint (favoring the band), and obscenity. Judge Gonzalez's obscenity ruling was overturned on appeal, and Florida's appeal to the United States Supreme Court was not granted. The Apellate opinion negating the finding of obscenity prevailed.

In the area of speech that would incite "imminent lawless action," the fighting words doctrine originated in the case *Brandenburg v. Ohio* [1969], two heavy metal artists were separately brought to court. Based on a 1985 incident, a case was brought in Nevada in 1988 that became known as *Vance v. Judas Priest*. The incident involved a suicide and suicide attempt by two young men while listening to Judas Priest's music. The complainants originally argued for a causal link between listening to the music and taking lawless action (suicide), invoking the fighting words doctrine. They later shifted their causal argument to the presence of "backmasked" messages urging "do it," and it became a product liability case, successfully fought by the band and their record label. The case known as *Waller v. Osbourne*, involving Ozzy Osbourne stayed with the "inciteful speech" argument. It ended when, in 1992, the Supreme Court declined to hear a final appeal of the case. The appellate court had overturned the finding of a causal link between listening and lawless action saying in part, "liability will only attach when the *intention* of dissemination was to cause the ensuing injury." That would mean thousands of suicides. Again, the musical artist prevailed—but not until after years of uncertainty over the possibility of an unfavorable outcome.

In the area of material "harmful to minors," it was the San Francisco punk band Dead Kennedys who were taken to court. It wasn't about the music on the band's third album *Fran-*

kenchrist, it had to do with an enclosed poster by renowned fantasy artist H.R. Giger. Despite a warning on the exterior of the package about potentially "shocking, repulsive, offensive" art within, the band was charged with distributing materials harmful to minors. Giger's "Landscape #20: Where Are We Coming From," described in court as showing "nine disembodied genital sex acts of a color and texture resembling armadillo skin" was the cause. It cost the band sixty thousand dollars of their own money to defend. They had no major label assistance, won the case, and broke up. Few cases involving popular music have been brought since these. Obscenity and inciteful speech proved difficult to argue successfully, but the "harm to minors" area of law is open to further probing. That is why this language has been thought viable in legislative proposals. Congress does not just pass laws. They have the power to investigate topics deemed important to their role in governing or that could lead to future legislation. . . .

It doesn't begin to detail activity in the fifty state legislatures. That is where the most dangerous legislative proposals specifically impacting popular music have been made in recent years. In 1989 Pennsylannia and Missouri considered mandatory record labeling laws and model legislation was circulated nationally in case it passed there. The 1992 Washington "erotic music" law discussed above was next. In 1998 Michigan looked at a concert-rating bill based on whether the concert artist's recorded product had been warning labeled in the previous five years. That would have required warning labels in concert ads. A bill was also proposed that would have allowed local authorities in towns with concert venues to declare some events "harmful to minors." Also in 1998 a Bill reached the floor in the Georgia state legislature, which borrowed language from the failed federal proposal to criminalize sale or rental of warning labeled product to minors. A similar bill was proposed, but never got out of committee in Tennessee that year. This front has been fairly quiet for several years but begs constant vigilance. . . .

The USA Patriot Act

There hasn't been much cause to examine the executive record on popular music, because it rarely goes beyond the level of popular culture bashing campaign rhetoric and [former President] Bill Clinton playing the saxophone. However, with the passage of the USA Patriot Act mentioned above, the United States' third branch of government has taken actions which could directly impact popular music as expression in this country. Passed by Congress on October 25th 2001 and signed into law by President George W. Bush the next day, this rapidly developed, 342-page bill couched in patriotic language, consolidated vast new powers with the Executive Branch. The vote in the House of Representatives was 357–66, the Senate's was 98–1, with only Russell Feingold, Democrat of Wisconsin, opposed. He said, in part, "I have concluded that this bill does not strike the right balance between empowering law enforcement and protecting civil liberties. . . ."

Limiting discussion here to aspects of USA Patriot that could impact popular music, one must begin with Section 802 that creates a federal crime known as "domestic terrorism," which covers "acts dangerous to human life that are a violation of the criminal laws" if they "appear to be intended . . . to influence the policy of a government by intimidation or coercion," and if they "Occur primarily within the territorial jurisdiction of the United States." This can be construed to include public demonstrations and acts of civil disobedience, even nonviolent ones that protest against and seek to change government policies. Legal dissent. A march or rally, even with all required permits, with aggressive policing and crowd control, could precipitate behaviors that could create "dangers to human life" completely beyond the control of event organizers, raising the possibility of penalties applied under USA Patriot.

It is not hard to see that environmental, anti-globalization, or pro- and anti- abortion protesters could soon be labeled "domestic terrorists." What of musicians who perform at rallies that develop crowd control problems? The language of the Act considers "terrorist activities" to include soliciting membership, soliciting funds, or providing material support for any group declared "terrorist" by the government. If the musicians make statements supportive of the organization's aims or urge crowds to make donations in addition to the drawing power of their appearance, they could be individually prosecuted as domestic terrorists. Just by appearing they are providing a form of "material support" to the sponsoring organization, as would any cash donations. Also, the Executive Branch is not required to publicly list the organizations it considers "terrorist." Even tangential association with such a group could open musical artists up to increased surveillance of their telephone, e-mail, and internet traffic, as well as unannounced "sneak and peek" searches of their homes and offices. Such consequences could clearly lead to chilling effects on political speech by musicians and others. If they happen to be non-citizens, the consequences can be even more dire. . . .

Popular music is integral to the United States' contributions to the world culture and deserves the full protection the Constitution provides.

Despite repeated and ongoing instances of opposition to unfettered musical expression in the United States, I do not believe there is a coordinated nationwide campaign being waged against it. Anti-music alliances ebb and flow, but do not seem consistently organized. However, I do see steady, even increasing pressure by some with governmental power to restrict or regulate aspects of popular music, which are offensive to them. Prior to USA Patriot, the courts provided an effective, if slow and frightening counterbalance to the excesses of legislative and prosecutorial zeal. Whether they remain so in spite of changes in law like USA Patriot or composition of the Supreme Court will only be known in the fullness of time. My prescription for this state of affairs remains unflagging observation and a willingness to fight unpopular battles when and if necessary. I'm afraid that day is coming. Those who fight such battles strive to protect the best that America could become through the open exchange of ideas through song. They are defending a progressive reading of the melting pot myth to facilitate the vigorous evolution of the musical expression of America's culture and artists. Popular song is a long acknowledged, beloved and protected vehicle of sociopolitical commentary and criticism. Songwriters and musicians do not hide behind the First Amendment, they stand proudly in front of it, trying to keep its protection of lyrics free and undiluted. Popular music is integral to the United States' contributions to world culture and deserves the full protection the Constitution provides.

More troubling at this time, is the movement of content-based regulation of popular music into the private realm. Corporations in the entertainment industry, especially music-oriented companies, have been put on notice that there could be consequences from government if their releases are offensive to some members of Congress. Through statements at Hearings and elevation of the stature of lobbyists who side with them on these issues, some legislators have added power and momentum to the activities of private pressure groups against free musical expression. They seem to be facilitating the assertion of a corporate ethic and aesthetic to constrain popular music content. From major retailers like Wal-Mart and K-Mart refusing to carry warning labeled products, to major labels divesting themselves of troublesome independent labels they distribute or have acquired, there have been ongoing effects. Tracks have been dropped from CD's or had their titles changed, some words have been silenced or electronically masked, and even package art has been changed, to guarantee access to all retail outlets. But, because these arrangements are being made voluntarily and privately, they are not prosecutable as censorship even if they have the same effect. . . .

One can only hope that the industry will not pander to the legislature's Puritans to gain favorable outcomes in other matters. The changes in law precipitated by USA Patriot have yet to be used in ways that permit meaningful forecasts regarding music and musicians. But, there are new threats to free expression abroad in the land, and music has not suddenly become immune. The worst case is that the foundations have been laid for a kinder, gentler, excuse me, compassionate, fascism. The private, voluntary corporate approach to content based regulation of music threatens to "dye the fabric" of American culture an unappealing, uniform shade of beige. Allowing our culture to be led by market forces and corporate morality could well be our downfall. It is an expression of a widespread American conceit that we think we're better than other nations and cultures, despite the fact that our mainstreamists are blind to the quality, contributions and impact of our popular music on a global scale.

If music artists continue to keep Americans and others honest about the ways and events of the world through critical commentary, life is good.

I do believe that American popular music is so directly a part of the lives and vitality of the people from whom the government's power derives (theoretically), that important non-mainstream voices will continue to be heard in our songs. The harm to minors line of legal reasoning is not yet fully played out and bears watching. But, cosmopolitan, world-aware popular musics are also abroad in the land. The formation of artists' rights groups like the Recording Artists' Coalition and sophisticated lobbying groups like the Future of

Music Coalition as pro-music advocates are encouraging responses in the current environment. If musical artists continue to keep Americans and others honest about the ways and events of the world through critical commentary, life is good. If lyric visionaries can continue to craft, record and release songs unencumbered by chilling effects and self-censorship imposed by market conditions, hope for better days can remain alive. Vigilance about the challenges and pitfalls facing our music and culture is the price of living in these interesting times.

3

Youths from Dysfunctional Families Identify with Violence in Lyrics

Mary Eberstadt

Mary Eberstadt is a research fellow at the Hoover Institution, a policy research center at Stanford University, and consulting editor to Policy Review, *the Hoover Institution's bimonthly journal. She is also author of* Home-Alone America: The Hidden Toll of Day Care, Behavioral Drugs, and Other Parent Substitutes.

Unlike yesterday's popular music, which rebelled against traditional values, the violence and exploitation of today's rock and rap music often reflect the psychological turmoil and damaging consequences that divorce and negligent or absent parents have on youths. The seemingly depraved, scathing lyrics of controversial recording artists often deal with the breakdown of the nuclear family. From the music of Kurt Cobain, the late grunge icon, to Pink, the "anti-Britney Spears" female artist, parental absence is explored through chaotic lyrics. Also, the misogyny in rapper Eminem's lyrics is leveled at his mother and ex-wife for being careless mothers, not at women in general. Consequently, it is not surprising that the rage in this generation's popular music is rooted in America's peaking divorce rate and weakened definitions of family.

Mary Eberstadt, "Eminem Is Right," *Policy Review*, December 2004–January 2005. Reproduced by permission. www.hoover.org/publications/policyreview/3432051.html.

If there is one subject on which the parents of America passionately agree, it is that contemporary adolescent popular music, especially the subgenres of heavy metal and hip-hop/rap, is uniquely degraded—and degrading—by the standards of previous generations. At first blush this seems slightly ironic. After all, most of today's baby-boom parents were themselves molded by rock and roll, bumping and grinding their way through adolescence and adulthood with legendary abandon. Even so, the parents are correct: Much of today's music *is* darker and coarser than yesterday's rock. Misogyny, violence, suicide, sexual exploitation, child abuse—these and other themes, formerly rare and illicit, are now as common as the surfboards, drive-ins, and sock hops of yesteryear.

In a nutshell, the ongoing adult preoccupation with current music goes something like this: *What is the overall influence of this deafening, foul, and often vicious-sounding stuff on children and teenagers?* This is a genuinely important question, and serious studies and articles, some concerned particularly with current music's possible link to violence, have lately been devoted to it. In 2000, the American Academy of Pediatrics, the American Medical Association, the American Psychological Association, and the American Academy of Child & Adolescent Psychiatry all weighed in against contemporary lyrics and other forms of violent entertainment before Congress with a first-ever "Joint Statement on the Impact of Entertainment Violence on Children."

Nonetheless, this is not my focus here. Instead, I would like to turn that logic about influence upside down and ask this question: *What is it about today's music, violent and disgusting though it may be, that resonates with so many American kids?*

As the reader can see, this is a very different way of inquiring about the relationship between today's teenagers and their music. The first question asks what the music does to adolescents; the second asks what it *tells* us about them. To answer that second question is necessarily to enter the roiling emotional waters in which that music is created and consumed—in other words, actually to listen to some of it and read the lyrics.

As it turns out, such an exercise yields a fascinating and little understood fact about today's adolescent scene. If yesterday's rock was the music of abandon, today's is that of abandon*ment*. The odd truth about contemporary teenage music—the characteristic that most separates it from what has gone before—is its compulsive insistence on the damage wrought by broken homes, family dysfunction, checked-out parents, and (especially) absent fathers. Papa Roach, Everclear, Blink-182, Good Charlotte, Eddie Vedder and Pearl Jam, Kurt Cobain and Nirvana, Tupac Shakur, Snoop Doggy Dogg, Eminem—these and other singers and bands, all of them award-winning top-40 performers who either are or were among the most popular icons in America, have their own generational answer to what ails the modern teenager. Surprising though it may be to some, that answer is dysfunctional childhood. Moreover, and just as interesting, many bands and singers explicitly link the most deplored themes in music today—suicide, misogyny, and drugs—with that lack of a quasi-normal, intact-home personal past.

American teenagers have enshrined a new generation of music idols whose shared generational signature in song after song is to rage about what not *having a nuclear family has done to them.*

To put this perhaps unexpected point more broadly, during the same years in which progressive-minded and politically correct adults have been excoriating Ozzie and Harriet [TV characters that embodied the traditional family] as an artifact of 1950s-style oppression, many millions of American teenagers have enshrined a new generation of music idols whose shared generational signature in song after song is to rage about what *not* having had a nuclear family has done to them. This is quite a fascinating puzzle of the times. The self-perceived emotional damage scrawled large across contemporary music may not be statistically quantifiable, but it is nonetheless among the most striking of all the unanticipated consequences of our home-alone world.

Demigods of Dysfunction

To begin with music particularly popular among white teenage boys, one best-selling example of broken-home angst is that of the "nu-metal" band known as Papa Roach and led by singer/songwriter "Coby Dick" Shaddix (dubbed by one reviewer the "prince of dysfunction"). Three members of that group, Coby Dick included, are self-identified children of divorce. In 2000, as critics noted at the time, their album *Infest* explored the themes of broken homes and child and teenage rage. The result was stunning commercial success: *Infest* sold more than 3 million copies. MTV.com explained why: "The pained, confessional songs struck a nerve with disenfranchised listeners who were tired of the waves of directionless aggression spewing from the mouths of other rap-rockers. They found kinship in Papa Roach songs like 'Broken Home' and 'Last Resort.'" . . .

Another band that climbed to the top of the charts recently is Everclear, led by singer Art Alexakis (also a child of divorce, as he has explained to interviewers). Like Papa Roach, Everclear/Alexakis explores the fallout of parental breakup not from the perspective of newly liberated adults, but from that of the child left behind who feels abandoned and betrayed. Several of Everclear's songs map this emotional ground in detail—from not wanting to meet mother's "new friends," to wondering how the father who walked out can sleep at night, to dreaming of that father coming back. In the song "Father of Mine," the narrator implores, "*take me back to the day /*

when I was still your golden boy." Another song, "Sick and Tired," explicitly links the anger-depression-suicide teen matrix to broken homes (as indeed do numerous other contemporary groups): "*I blame my family / their damage is living in me.*" . . .

Another group successfully working this tough emotional turf is chart-topping and multiple award-winning Blink-182, which grew out of the skateboard and snowboard scene to become one of the most popular bands in the country. As with Papa Roach and Everclear, the group's interest in the family breakdown theme is partly autobiographical: At least two members of the band say that their personal experiences as children of divorce have informed their lyrics. Blink-182's top-40 hit in 2001, "Stay Together for the Kids," is perhaps their best-known song (though not the only one) about broken homes. "*What stupid poem could fix this home*," the narrator wonders, adding, "*I'd read it every day.*" . . .

Then there is the phenomenon known as Pink, whose album *Missundaztood* was one of the top-10 albums of 2002, selling more than 3 million copies. Pink (dubbed by one writer the "anti-Britney") is extremely popular among young girls. Any teenager with a secular CD collection will likely own some of her songs. Pink mines the same troubled emotional territory as Blink-182 and numerous other bands, but even more exclusively: *Missundaztood* revolves entirely around the emotional wreckage and behavioral consequences of Pink's parents breaking up. A review of the album on ABCnews.com noted, *Missundaztood* is full of painful tales of childhood—divorce, rebellion, disaffection and drugs. It's the stuff that may make parents shake their heads, but causes millions of alienated kids to nod in approval." In Pink's especially mournful (and perhaps best-known) song, "Family Portrait," the narrator repeatedly begs her father not to leave, offering even the pitiful childish enticement, "*I won't spill the milk at dinner.*"

Yet another popular group generating anthem after anthem about broken homes and their consequences is Washington, D.C.-area–based Good Charlotte, profiled on the cover of *Rolling Stone* in May 2003 as the "Polite Punks." Their first album went gold in 2002. Led by twins Benji and Joel Madden, whose father walked out one Christmas Eve and never returned, Good Charlotte is one band that would not even exist except for the broken homes in which three of its four members (guitarist Billy Martin being the third) grew up. The twins have repeatedly told interviewers it was that trauma that caused them to take up music in the first place, and family breakup figures repeatedly in Good Charlotte's songs and regularly shapes its stage appearances and publicity. (In a particular act of symbolic protest, the twins recently made the legal changeover to their mother's maiden name.) . . .

These songs reflect the zeitgeist of an age group coping with the highest marital-breakdown rate ever recorded in America.

Papa Roach, Everclear, Blink-182, Pink, Good Charlotte: These bands are only some of the top-40 groups now supplying the teenage demand for songs about dysfunctional and adult abandoned homes. In a remarkable 2002 article published in the pop music magazine *Blender* (remarkable because it lays out in detail what is really happening in today's metal/grunge/punk/rock music), an award-winning music journalist named William Shaw listed several other bands, observing, "If there's a theme running through rock at the beginning of the twenty-first century, it's a pervasive sense of hurt. For the past few years, bands like Korn, Linkin Park, Slip-knot, Papa Roach, and Disturbed have been thrusting forward their dark accounts of dysfunctional upbringings. . . . As the clichéd elder might mutter, what's wrong with kids today?" Shaw answers his own question this way: "[T]hese songs reflect the zeitgeist of an age group coping with the highest marital-breakdown rate ever recorded in America. If this era's music says anything, it's that this generation sees itself as uniquely fractured."

As he further observes, so powerful are the emotions roused in fans by these songs that stars and groups themselves are often surprised by it. Shaw relates the following about "Coby Dick" Shaddix of Papa Roach, who wrote the aforementioned song "Broken Home": "He's become used to [fans] coming up and telling him, over and over 'You know that song "Broken Home?" That's my f--- life, right there.' 'It's a bit sad that that's true, you know?' [Shaddix] says." Similarly, singer Chad Kroeger of Nickelback reports of a hit song he wrote on his own abandonment by his father at age two. "You should see some people who I meet after shows. . . . They break down weeping, and they're like, 'I went through the exact same thing!' Sometimes it's terrifying how much they relate to it." That Nickelback hit song, titled "Too Bad," laments that calling *"from time to time / To make sure we're alive"* just isn't enough.

Shaw's ultimate conclusion is an interesting one that this emphasis in current music on abandoned children represents an unusually loaded form of teenage rebellion. "This is the sound of one generation reproaching another—only this time, it's the scorned, world-weary children telling off their narcissistic, irresponsible parents," he writes. "[Divorce] could be rock's ideal subject matter. These are songs about the chasm in understanding between parents—who routinely don't comprehend the grief their children are feeling—and children who don't know why their parents have torn up their world."

That is a sharp observation. Also worth noting is this historical point: The same themes of adult absence and child abandonment have been infiltrating hard rock even longer than these current bands have been around—probably for as long as family breakup rates began accelerating.

Both musically and emotionally, many of today's groups owe much to the example of the late grunge-rock idol Kurt Cobain, who prefigured today's prominent themes both autobiographically and otherwise. A star whose personal life has legendary status for his fans, Cobain was a self-described happy child until his parents' divorce when he was seven. The years following were a miserable blur of being shuffled around to grandparents and other caretakers, including a spate of homelessness. The rage and frustration of that experience appear in some of Cobain's famously nihilistic lyrics, including the early song "Sliver," about a boy kicking and screaming upon being dropped off elsewhere by Mom and Dad yet again. The later, markedly cynical "Serve the Servants" reflects on how his traumatic childhood became exploited for personal gain. As with Cobain, so, too, with his friend Pearl Jam singer Eddie Vedder. For more than a decade Pearl Jam has reigned as one of the best-known bands in current rock, and Vedder as one of the most adulated singers; indeed, the band's distinctive sound commands instant recognition among almost every American under the age of 30 with working ears. And Pearl Jam, like the aforementioned groups, has achieved that success, according to Vedder, partly because of the group's frankness about the costs of fractured families and about related themes of alienation and suicide. . . .

Where's Daddy?

Even less recognized than the white music emphasis on broken homes and the rest of the dysfunctional themes is that the popular black-dominated genres, particularly hip-hop/rap, also reflect themes of abandonment, anger, and longing for parents. Interestingly enough, this is true of particular figures whose work is among the most adult deplored.

Once again, when it comes to the deploring part, critics have a point. It is hard to imagine a more unwanted role model (from the parental point of view) than the late Tupac

Shakur. A best-selling gangsta rapper who died in a shoot-out in 1996 at age 25 (and the object of a 2003 documentary called *Tupac: Resurrection*), Shakur was a kind of polymath of criminality. In the words of a *Denver Post* review of the movie, "In a perfect circle of life imitating art originally meant to imitate life, Shakur in 1991 began a string of crimes that he alternately denied and reveled in. He claimed Oakland police beat him up in a jaywalking arrest, later shot two off-duty cops, assaulted a limo driver and video directors, and was shot five times in a robbery." Further, "At the time of his drive-by murder in Law [Las] Vegas, he was out on bail pending appeal of his conviction for sexual abuse of a woman who charged him with sodomy in New York." . . .

It is hard to find a rapper who does not sooner or later invoke a dead or otherwise long-absent father.

Yet Shakur—who never knew his father and whose mother, a long time drug addict, was arrested for possession of crack when he was a child—is provocative in another, quite overlooked way. He is the author of some of the saddest lyrics in the hip-hop/gangsta-rap pantheon, which is saying quite a lot. To sophisticated readers familiar with the observations about the breakup of black families recorded several decades ago in the Moynihan Report [a 1965 report headed by Senator Daniel Patrick Moynihan that identifies the legacies of slavery, urbanization, discrimination, and matriarchy as reasons why many black families suffer crises] and elsewhere, the fact that so many young black men grow up without fathers may seem so well established as to defy further comment. But evidently some young black men—Shakur being one—see things differently. In fact, it is hard to find a rapper who does not sooner or later invoke a dead or otherwise long-absent father, typically followed by the hope that he will not become such a man himself. Or there is the flip side of that unintended bow to the nuclear family, which is the hagiography [idealization] in some rappers' lyrics of their mothers.

In a song called "Papa'z Song Lyrics," Shakur opens with the narrator imagining his father showing up after a long absence, resulting in an expletive-laden tirade. The song then moves to a lacerating description of growing up fatherless that might help to explain why Shakur is an icon not only to many worse-off teenagers from the ghetto, but also to many better-off suburban ones. Here is a boy who "*had to play catch by myself*," who prays: "*Please send me a pops before puberty.*"

The themes woven together in this song—anger, bitterness, longing for family, misogyny as the consequence of a world without fathers—make regular appearances in some other rappers' lyrics, too. One is Snoop Doggy Dogg, perhaps the preeminent rapper of the 1990s. Like Shakur and numerous other rappers, his personal details cause many a parent to shudder; since his childhood he has been arrested for a variety of crimes, including cocaine possession (which resulted in three years of jail service), accomplice to murder (for which he was acquitted), and, most recently, marijuana possession. ("It's not my job to stop kids doing the wrong thing, it's their parents' job," he once explained to a reporter.) In a song called "Mama Raised Me," sung with Soulja Slim, Snoop Doggy Dogg offers this explanation of how troubled pasts come to be: "*It's probably pop's fault how I ended up / Gangbangin'; crack slangin'; not givin' a f---.*"

Another black rapper who returned repeatedly to the theme of father abandonment is Jay-Z, also known as Shawn Carter, whose third and breakthrough album, *Hard Knock Life*, sold more than 500,000 copies. He also has a criminal history (he says he had been a cocaine dealer) and a troubled family history, which is reflected in his music. In an interview with MTV.com about his latest album, the reporter explained: "Jay and his father had been estranged until earlier this year [2003]. [His father] left the household and his family's life (Jay has an older brother and two sisters) when Shawn was just 12 years old. The separation had served as a major 'block' for Jay over the years. . . . His most vocal tongue lashing toward his dad was on the *Dynasty: Roc la Familia* cut 'Where Have You Been,' where he rapped 'F--- you very much / You showed me the worst kind of pain.'"

The fact that child abandonment is also a theme in hip-hop might help explain what otherwise appears as a commercial puzzle—namely, how this particular music moved from the fringes of black entertainment to the very center of the Everyteenager mainstream. There can be no doubt about the current social preeminence of these black- and ghetto-dominated genres in the lives of many better-off adolescents, black *and* white. As Donna Britt wrote in a *Washington Post* column noting hip-hop's ascendancy, "In modern America, where urban based hip hop culture dominates music, fashion, dance and, increasingly, movies and TV, these kids are trendsetters. What they feel, think and do could soon play out in a middle school—or a Pottery Barn–decorated bedroom—near you."

Eminem: Reasons for Rage

A final example of the rage in contemporary music against irresponsible adults—perhaps the most interesting—is that of genre-crossing bad-boy rap superstar Marshall Mathers or Eminem (sometime stage persona "Slim Shady"). Of all the names guaranteed to send a shudder down the parental spine, his is probably the most effective. In fact, Eminem has single-handedly, if inadvertently, achieved the otherwise ideologically impossible: He is the object of a vehemently disapproving public consensus shared by the National Organization for Women, the Gay & Lesbian Alliance Against Defamation, [politician and writer] William J. Bennett, Lynne Cheney [wife of vice president Dick Cheney and a scholar and author], [news commentator] Bill O'Reilly, and a large number of other social conservatives as well as feminists and gay activists. In sum, this rapper—"as harmful to America as any al Qaeda fanatic," in O'Reilly's opinion—unites adult polar opposites as perhaps no other single popular entertainer has done.

There is small need to wonder why. Like other rappers, Eminem mines the shock value and gutter language of rage, casual sex, and violence. Unlike the rest, however, he appears to be a particularly attractive target of opprobrium [contempt] for two distinct reasons. One, he is white and therefore politically easier to attack. (It is interesting to note that black rappers have not been targeted by name anything like Eminem has.) Perhaps even more important, Eminem is one of the largest commercially visible targets for parental wrath. Wildly popular among teenagers these last several years, he is also enormously successful in commercial terms. Winner of numerous Grammys and other music awards and a perpetual nominee for many more, he has also been critically (albeit reluctantly) acclaimed for his acting performance in the autobiographical 2003 movie *8 Mile.* For all these reasons, he is probably the preeminent rock/rap star of the last several years, one whose singles, albums, and videos routinely top every chart. His 2002 album, *The Eminem Show*, for example, was easily the most successful of the year, selling more than 7.6 million copies.

This remarkable market success, combined with the intense public criticism that his songs have generated, makes the phenomenon of Eminem particularly intriguing. Perhaps more than any other current musical icon, he returns repeatedly to the same themes that fuel other success stories in contemporary music: parental loss, abandonment, abuse, and subsequent child and adolescent anger, dysfunction, and violence (including self-violence). Both in his raunchy lyrics as well as in *8 Mile*, Mathers's own personal story has been parlayed many times over: the absent father, the troubled mother living in a trailer park, the series of unwanted maternal boyfriends, the protective if impotent feelings toward a younger sibling (in the movie, a baby sister; in real life, a younger brother), and the fine line that a poor, ambitious, and unguided young man might walk between catastrophe and success. Mathers plumbs these and related themes with a verbal savagery that leaves most adults aghast.

Yet Eminem also repeatedly centers his songs on the crypto-traditional notion that children need parents and that *not* having them has made all hell break loose. In the song "8 Mile" from the movie soundtrack, for example, the narrator studies his little sister as she colors one picture after another of an imagined nuclear family, failing to understand that "*mommas got a new man.*" "*Wish I could be the daddy that neither one of us had,*" he comments. Such wistful lyrics juxtapose oddly and regularly with Eminem's violent other lines. Even in one of his most infamous songs, "Cleaning Out My Closet (Mama, I'm Sorry)," what drives the vulgar narrative is the insistence on seeing abandonment from a child's point of view. "*My faggot father must have had his panties up in a bunch / 'Cause he split. I wonder if he even kissed me good-bye.*"

Contrary to what critics have intimated, misogyny in current music does not spring from nowhere; it is often linked to the larger theme of having been abandoned.

As with other rappers, the vicious narrative treatment of women in some of Eminem's songs is part of this self-conception as a child victim. Contrary to what critics have intimated, the misogyny in current music does not spring from nowhere; it is often linked to the larger theme of having been abandoned several times—left behind by father, not nurtured by mother, and betrayed again by faithless womankind. One of the most violent and sexually aggressive songs in the last few years is "Kill You" by the popular metal band known as Korn. Its violence is not directed toward just any woman or even toward the narrator's girlfriend; it is instead a song about an abusive stepmother whom the singer imagines going back to rape and murder.

Similarly, Eminem's most shocking lyrics about women are not randomly dispersed; they are largely reserved for his mother and ex-wife, and the narrative pose is one of despising them for not being better women—in particular, better mothers. The worst rap directed at his own mother is indeed gut-wrenching: "*But how dare you try to take what you didn't help me to get? / You selfish bitch, I hope you f--- burn in hell for this shit!*" It is no defense of the gutter to observe the obvious: This is not the expression of random misogyny but, rather, of primal rage over alleged maternal abdication and abuse. . . .

Sex, Drugs, Rock and Roll, and Broken Homes

To say that today's popular music is uniquely concerned with broken homes, abandoned children, and distracted or incapable parents is not to say that this is what all of it is about. Other themes remain a constant, too, although somewhat more brutally than in the alleged golden era recalled by some baby boomers.

Much of today's metal and hip-hop, like certain music of yesterday, romanticizes illicit drug use and alcohol abuse, and much of current hip-hop sounds certain radical political themes, such as racial separationism and violence against the police. And, of course, the most elementally appealing feature of all, the sexually suggestive beat itself, continues to lure teenagers and young adults in its own right—including those from happy homes. Today as yesterday, plenty of teenagers who don't know or care what the stars are raving about find enough satisfaction in swaying to the sexy music. As professor and intellectual Allan Bloom observed about rock in his best-seller, *The Closing of the American Mind* (Simon & Schuster, 1987), the music "gives children, on a silver platter, with all the public authority of the entertaining industry, everything their parents always used to tell them they had to wait for until they grew up and would understand later."

Even so, and putting aside such obvious continuities with previous generations, there is no escaping the fact that today's songs are musically and lyrically unlike any before. What distinguishes them most clearly is a fixation on having been abandoned personally by the adults supposedly in charge, with consequences ranging from bitterness to rage to bad, sick, and violent behavior.

Today's teenagers and their music rebel against their parents because they are not *parents—not nurturing, not attentive, and often not even there.*

And therein lies a painful truth about an advantage that many teenagers of yesterday enjoyed but their own children often do not. Baby boomers and their music rebelled against parents *because* they were parents—nurturing, attentive, and overly present (as those teenagers often saw it) authority figures. Today's teenagers and their music rebel against parents because they are *not* parents—not nurturing, not attentive, and often not even there. This difference in generational experience may not lend itself to statistical measure, but it is as real as the platinum and gold records that continue to capture it. What those records show compared to yesteryear's rock is emotional downward mobility. Surely if some of the current generation of teenagers and young adults had been better taken care of, then the likes of Kurt Cobain, Eminem, Tupac Shakur, and certain other parental nightmares would have been mere footnotes to recent music history rather than rulers of it.

To step back from the emotional immediacy of those lyrics and to juxtapose the ascendance of such music alongside the long-standing sophisticated assaults on what is sardonically called "family values" is to meditate on a larger irony. As today's music stars and their raving fans likely do not know, many commentators and analysts have been rationalizing every aspect of the adult exodus from home—sometimes celebrating it full throttle, as in the example of working motherhood—longer than most of today's singers and bands have been alive.

Nor do they show much sign of second thoughts. Representative sociologist Stephanie Coontz greeted the year 2004 with one more op-ed piece aimed at burying poor metaphorical Ozzie and Harriet for good. She reminded America again that "changes in marriage and family life" are here to stay and aren't "necessarily a problem"; that what is euphemistically called "family diversity" is or ought to be cause for celebration. Many other scholars and observers—to say nothing of much of polite adult society—agree with Coontz. Throughout the contemporary nonfiction literature written of, by, and for educated adults, a thousand similar rationalizations about family "changes" bloom on.

Meanwhile, a small number of emotionally damaged former children, embraced and adored by millions of teenagers like them, rage on in every commercial medium available about the multiple damages of the disappearance of loving, protective, attentive adults—and they reap a fortune for it. If this spectacle alone doesn't tell us something about the ongoing emotional costs of parent-child separation on today's outsize scale, it's hard to see what could.

4

Lyrics with Violence Should Not Be Protected by the First Amendment

John F. Borowski

John F. Borowski is an environmental and marine science teacher in North Salem High School in Oregon.

Explicit and violent lyrics in music, especially those of popular rap "artists" who objectify, abuse, and debase women—should not be protected by the First Amendment and should be subject to limitations. Young, impressionable listeners often adopt skewed views of inner-city life and misogynistic, materialistic attitudes through rap lyrics that glorify "pimping," or profiting from the prostitution of marginalized, poor young women. Therefore, the self-aggrandizing, sexist language of these "antiheroes" of popular music must be challenged in schools, at home, and by defenders of free speech.

Students bring to school the latest youth jargon, a rite of passage for every generation. These newest semantics though are building a foundation of slang, so vile, so degrading that even the most cynic critic of adolescent "speak" will cringe. But "the race to the bottom" in terms of communication is setting a dangerous precedent where debasement of women is just and the glorification of those who bastardize them is acceptable.

John F. Borowski, "Pimping the First Amendment," *CommonDreams.org*, October 16, 2004. Reproduced by permission. www.commondreams.org/views04/1016-29.htm.

[Rapper] "50 Cent" a supposed music "artist" was recently heralded for his musical achievements in the medium of "music videos." Mind you, having grown up in Northern New Jersey and having all my family in the Bronx and Queens, I thought I had heard it all. Now, as a teacher I will encounter the glorification of "50 Cent" in my school and maybe, even be treated to a favorite verse by teenagers parodying their hero. "Ho make the pimp rich, I ain't payin' bitch."

"50 Cent" and [rapper] "Snoop Dogg" are leading children into a duplicitous lie, where pimps are some perverse antihero, as if the business of procuring women and girls as prostitutes for profit is acceptable. Now in school, I must stop each student I hear discussing "bitch slappin" or "big pimpin" and give them a dose of reality of what those terms mean. Words are our means of communication, words carry impact and value and can scar and maim. Some defenders of this genre will hide behind the First Amendment. Freedom of speech comes with a price and that price is meant to benefit society. Try yelling bomb in an airport and see how free speech has limitations: for the good of the community rather than the individual. As a die-hard defender of the First Amendment, I would dishonor the framers' intentions of free speech if I allowed this language to go unchallenged in and out of school.

After kicking around as an ironworker, laborer and other assorted jobs, I found my niche as a teacher. During a trip to New York City, I was propositioned by a sex worker, or as some would call a ho. She was a beautiful African American woman, who was articulate and witty. During conversation, she told me that her parents had thrown her out of her house, professionals that ironically, worked in the same neighborhood I taught in. I gave her twenty dollars, told her to get a bus home and make up with her parents. Her eyes welled up and she hugged me and kissed my cheek and simply said, "thanks." She told me no one on the street had every shown her any concern, unless a sexual act was part of the deal. I think of her from time to time, knowing that she probably didn't meet the fate of Julia Roberts in *Pretty Woman* [whose character, a prostitute, is transformed by a wealthy businessman]. No, her world, now mocked by those who write lyrics about her pain probably had a wall of obstacles: a world of being subhuman, having no rights or being invisible.

The average entry into prostitution is thirteen years old, just like the kids I will have in my science class and the age of my youngest daughter. The prevalence of incest among these girls and boys that enter prostitution runs between 65 percent to 90 percent and about 90 percent of all prostitutes have pimps, those glorious men in the big rimmed hats and fur coats that now are fashionable. The rate of rape reported by prostitutes hovers around 80 percent, with some girls raped eight to ten times per year: so much for the oldest trade in the world as being victimless. Add to this the rate of violence mainly by pimps, from broken arms to burnings with cigarettes and you may understand why I shudder when I hear a girl called a ho in school.

Everything Is for Sale

We are letting our children's childhoods evaporate, leaving them to navigate the shark-filled waters of our new "everything is for sale" society. Many young girls will be wearing their September best for school: thongs for preteens called "eye candy," overpriced shirts bearing a meaningless logo and listening to the numbing beat of music where profanity replaces creativity as adjectives. Their hallways are a verbal minefield where their appearance is judged and juried, but don't worry, they can drown their sorrows in a can of Pepsi provided by the school. Corporate pimps look to make kids hyper acute of themselves, where only self-indulgence and materialism are the placebos of medicating their self-doubt, inhibitions and fears. "Logomania" be it empty, profane verses of a song or an empty promise made in a corporate come-on can never fulfill a child like the love of a caring adult, the respect given by a peer or the knowledge of one's self worth minus the glitz. This is no time to be obsequious lapdogs to those who look to "pimp" our children: no, it is time to find our internal resolve and show some moral courage.

The terms pimp or bitch have no place in school. For those who glorify such scum, I suggest society give them a square kick in the buttocks. If "Snoop Dogg" and his ilk are artists who care about the condition of inner city children, provide financial support to organizations that will give women a hand up, not a "bitch slap." Sing about the true nature of pimps: the underbelly of society who should be an endangered species made extinct. Revel in the qualities that define one's worth: no gaudy medallion or gratuitous T-shirt can give cover to your shallowness.

Don't buy into the perverted spin that casts debasement be it in a song or video as free speech.

Teachers, refuse to have those words used in your class or hallways. Take time to explain what a pimp really is and how women do not cherish being sex workers: give your students a dose of reality. Reach out to those who are despondent, because the end of a rope or the edge of a razor may be their final solution to perceived insurmountable problems. Parents listen to what your children call music and have a loving discussion about the boundaries of what is acceptable and why.

Columbia Pictures, which plans to release an eighty-minute cartoon about a nine-year old pimp, should feel your wrath. Does our society have a place for kids reveling in "lil' pimp T-shirts" or playing out fantasies on a pimp board game? Don't buy into the perverted spin that casts debasement be it in song or video as free speech. Call it for what it is: pawning children for profit, no matter the cost.

I will find myself humming to a rap song when I greet my students. Called "I Can" by "Nas," it focuses on what children can be and should be, no exploitation, no false illusions about what determines their beauty as humans. "I know I can, be what I want to be. If I work hard at it, I'll be where I want to be."

The question is where are we as adults, as the wise elders who must lead? Do we know what we can be? Fifty-five million school children await our decisions.

5

The Recording Industry Should Take Responsibility for Violence in Lyrics

Michael Rich

Michael Rich is a pediatrician and a member of the American Academy of Pediatrics.

Although scientific studies have failed to prove that violent and exploitative lyrics in music are direct causes of negative behaviors or violent acts, the recording industry should take more measures to prevent susceptible young consumers from being exposed to inappropriate content. Popular music plays a role in how adolescents shape their identities and attitudes, and because censorship is not desirable, the recording industry and retailers should devise a system that identifies the contents in music and makes lyrics readily accessible. Moreover, artists and broadcasters should show sensitivity in the content they produce, perform, or air, and the recording industry should place more encouragement on child-positive music.

My name is Michael Rich, and I am testifying on behalf of the American Academy of Pediatrics (AAP) and its 57,000 pediatrician members. I am a member of the Academy's Committee on Public Education. I practice pediatrics and adolescent medicine at Children's Hospital Boston, and teach

Michael Rich, "Prepared Witness Testimony, Recording Industry Marketing Practices: A Check-Up, Subcommittee on Telecommunications and the Internet," October 1, 2002. http://energycommerce.house.gov/reparchives/107/hearings/10012002Hearing718/Rich1203.htm.

at Harvard Medical School and Harvard School of Public Health. In my research, I study the effects of various entertainment media on the physical and mental health of children and adolescents. I actually began my professional career as a filmmaker. I love audiovisual media and continue to work in video and radio production, developing pro-child and health-positive media as tools for child health research, education, and advocacy. Finally, and most importantly, I am the father of a 16-year-old daughter and a 14-year-old son.

Parents alone cannot stem the tidal wave of images their children are exposed to throughout a given day. They need help, particularly from the entertainment industry and retailers.

Impact of Media on Health and Behavior of Children

Starting from when we are very young, we get the majority of our information from media, which includes television, movies, music, magazines, the Internet, video games, books, videos and all forms of advertising. While media offers us, including children, many opportunities to learn and to be entertained, how people interpret media images and media messages also can be a contributing factor to a variety of public health concerns. Among children and adolescents, research shows that key areas of concern are:

- Aggressive behavior and violence; desensitization to violence, both public and personal
- Substance abuse and use
- Nutrition, obesity and dieting
- Sexuality, body image and self-concept
- Advertising, marketing and consumerism

As a result of this research, the AAP and its members have been working on many fronts to help parents and children glean the best from unending media exposure. The AAP launched its Media Matters campaign (www.aap.org/advocacy/mediamatters.htm) years ago [in 1997] to help pediatricians, other health professionals, parents and children become more knowledgeable about the impact that media messages can have on children's health behaviors. Public education brochures on the media have been developed and distributed, including one that explains how the various ratings systems work. In addition, the Academy established a Media Resource Team (www.aap.org/mrt) in 1994 to work with the entertainment industry in providing the latest and most accurate information relating to the health and well being of infants, children, adolescents and young adults.

Parents alone cannot stem the tidal wave of images their children are exposed to throughout a given day. They need help, particularly from the entertainment industry and retailers.

Impact of Music Lyrics and Music Videos

Pediatricians' concern about the impact of music lyrics and music videos on children and youth compelled the American Academy of Pediatrics to issue a policy statement on the subject 13 years ago, with revised, updated versions developed and published multiple times since then. Policy statements communicate the official position of the Academy concerning health care issues, and help guide pediatricians in their assessment and treatment of patients.

As a pediatrician who specializes in adolescent medicine, I am keenly aware of how crucial music is to a teen's identity and how it helps them define important social and interpersonal behaviors. In fact, one study showed that 24% of high school students ranked popular music as one of their top 3 sources for guidance on social interaction. We often use music to define our beliefs and convictions. We are attracted to music that will confirm and support these beliefs and convictions. Music can truly affirm and confirm a teenager's struggles, joys, sorrows, fears, and fantasies.

During the past four decades, rock music lyrics have become increasingly explicit—particularly with reference to drugs, sex, violence and sexual violence. Heavy metal and rap lyrics have elicited the greatest concern, as they compound the environment in which some adolescents increasingly are confronted with risk-taking, substance use, pregnancy, HIV/AIDS and other sexually transmitted diseases, homicide and suicide.

With the advent of MTV and VH-1, not only do we have to listen to violent lyrics, but we also get to see violent narratives graphically portrayed.

Despite stories in the popular press relating suicides, ritualistic killings and school shootings to popular music influence, to date, no scientific studies have proved a cause-and-effect relationship between violent or sexually explicit lyrics and adverse behavioral effects. Causality is exceedingly difficult to prove, as we have all witnessed in the debate about whether tobacco smoking causes lung cancer, heart disease, and stroke. However, all of us, pediatricians, parents, and responsible members of society, must pay attention to the associations that have been observed between music content and health outcomes. There is some music that communicates potentially harmful health messages, especially when it reaches a vulnerable and impressionable audience. Teenagers become absorbed in songs they believe help better define them during this rocky transition into adulthood. The words and images evoked by popular music are powerful influences on how they are socialized. Youth who feel rejected and alienated are especially responsive to lyrics that glorify hostility and violence. Numerous studies indicate that a preference for heavy metal music may be a significant marker for alienation, substance abuse, psychiatric disorders, suicide risk, sex-role stereotyping, or risk-taking behaviors during adolescence. With the advent of MTV and VH-1, not only do we have to listen to violent lyrics, but we also get to see violent narratives graphically portrayed. Research studies indicate that music videos may have a significant behavioral impact by increasing violent attitudes and behaviors in viewers, desensitizing male college students to violence against women, disproportionately reinforcing racial and gender stereotypes, and by making teenagers more likely to accept and engage in unsafe sex.

The world can be a threatening and scary place, especially for young people who feel powerless, disenfranchised, or disrespected due to economics, race, or beliefs. Artists should have the right to reflect that reality and address any issue in any way that they choose. However, we must recognize that the content that we choose to listen to inevitably affects us and we must choose accordingly. Changes in young people's attitudes and behaviors toward each other hurt all young people, regardless of their race, gender, religious or ethnic backgrounds. Parents and pediatricians believe that it is important to know the contents of the food we feed our children's bodies. To protect their physical and mental health, we should be equally aware of what, to paraphrase [rock band] Jefferson Airplane, we feed their heads.

AAP Recommendations

Although there is no one solution, awareness of and sensitivity to the potential impact of music lyrics and videos by consumers, the entertainment and music industry is one important piece of the puzzle. It is in children's and teenagers' best interest to listen to lyrics or to watch videos that are not violent, sexist, drug-oriented, or antisocial. As a result, the Academy has, in our November 2001 policy statement on media violence, suggested that "music lyrics should be made easily available to parents so that they can read before deciding whether to purchase the recording." To date, this has not occurred. Many recordings are broadcasted in sanitized radio versions, which are difficult, if not impossible, to buy retail. The current system of parental advisory labels applied by the producers themselves provides inadequate information for parents to make appropriate choices for their children. To disclose the content of their product is not a violation of rights, but truth in advertising.

The entertainment industry should extend personal concern for the well being of children to their business of creating and selling music.

The Academy strongly opposes censorship. We advocate for more child-positive media. As a society, we have to acknowledge the responsibility that parents, the music industry and others have in helping to foster the nation's children. The entertainment industry should extend personal concern for the well being of children to their business of creating and selling music, movies, television programming and video games.

Although the evidence is incomplete, based on our knowledge of child and adolescent development, the AAP believes that the public, including the recording industry and parents, should be aware of pediatricians' concerns about the possible negative impact of music lyrics and videos. The Academy recommends that:

- The music industry should develop and apply a system of specific content labeling of music regarding violence, sex, drugs, or offensive lyrics. We label the food we eat—why not label the music? Let the consumer, including parents and youth, know what the music contains and let the educated consumer make the decision. For those concerned about the "forbidden fruit" syndrome, one study has examined the impact of parental advisory labels, and it found that teens were not more likely to be attracted simply because of the labeling.

- Music lyrics should be made easily available to parents so that they can read before deciding whether to purchase the recording.
- Broadcasters and the music industry should be encouraged to demonstrate sensitivity and self-restraint in decisions regarding what is produced, marketed and broadcast.
- Performers should be encouraged to serve as positive role models for children and teenagers.
- Research should be developed concerning the impact music lyrics have on the behavior of adolescents and preadolescents.
- Parents should take an active role in monitoring music that their children are exposed to and which they can purchase, as well as the videos they watch. Ultimately, it is the parent's responsibility to monitor what their children listen to and view. Pediatricians should encourage parents to do so.
- Pediatricians should counsel parents to become educated about the media. In order to help this process, the Academy has launched Media Matters, a national media education campaign targeted to physicians, parents and youth. The primary goal of the Media Matters campaign is to help parents and children understand and protect themselves against the sometimes negative effects of images and messages in the media, including music lyrics and videos.

Media education includes developing critical thinking and viewing skills, and offering creative alternatives to media consumption. The Academy is particularly concerned about entertainment media images and messages, and the resulting impact on the health of vulnerable young people, in areas including violence, safety, sexuality, use of alcohol, tobacco, and illicit drugs, nutrition, and self-concept and identity.

For example, if a music video shows violence against women to any degree, a viewer, including young girls, could be led to believe such action is acceptable. If they were educated about the media, the premise in the video would be questioned and hopefully rejected.

Parents should also be reminded that if we, as consumers, do not buy or use entertainment media that are harmful to children, these media would no longer be produced. Media are not the only cause of violence, sexism, racism, or health risk behaviors, but they are a powerful influence on these behaviors over which we have some control.

There must be a collective solution to this social problem. Parents, pediatricians, the music industry and others have critical roles in discussing and addressing the increasing amount of violence in society, particularly when it comes to children and adolescents. If we can make our lives and our future safer by paying attention to these issues and intervening where necessary, then we owe it to our children, ourselves, and our society to do so.

6

Hip-Hop and Rap Lyrics Contain Gratuitous Violence and Cause Harm

John H. McWhorter

John H. McWhorter is a senior fellow at the Manhattan Institute, a political and economic research organization. He is the author of several books, including Winning the Race: Beyond the Crisis in Black America, Doing Our Own Thing: The Degradation of Language *and* Music in America and Why We Should, Like, Care.

The lyrics in rap and hip-hop music glorify violence, criminality, and misogyny, perpetuating detrimental stereotypes of—and models of behavior for—African American youths. This crass genre of popular music is dominated by rappers with criminal records who flaunt their inclination for lawlessness, materialism, and antisocial behaviors and attitudes, whom many young African Americans idolize and emulate. The defense that exploitative, violent rap and hip-hop lyrics are a brutal testament of inner-city life and consequences of racism, and that rap and hip-hop artists meaningfully represent the struggle of African Americans, is ill-informed and misleading. On the contrary, rap and hip-hop culture does nothing to elevate African American communities, instead exacerbating their long-standing crises: poverty, crime, illiteracy, and institutionalized racism.

John H. McWhorter, "How Hip-hop Holds Blacks Back," *City Journal*, Summer 2003. Reproduced by permission. www.city-journal.org/html/13_3_how_hip_hop.html.

Not long ago, I was having lunch in a KFC in Harlem, sitting near eight African-American boys, aged about 14. Since 1) it was 1:30 on a school day, 2) they were carrying book bags, and 3) they seemed to be in no hurry, I assumed they were skipping school. They were extremely loud and unruly, tossing food at one another and leaving it on the floor.

Black people ran the restaurant and made up the bulk of the customers, but it was hard to see much healthy "black community" here. After repeatedly warning the boys to stop throwing food and keep quiet, the manager finally told them to leave. The kids ignored her. Only after she called a male security guard did they start slowly making their way out, tauntingly circling the restaurant before ambling off. These teens clearly weren't monsters, but they seemed to consider themselves exempt from public norms of behavior—as if they had begun to check out of mainstream society.

What struck me most, though, was how fully the boys' music—hard-edged rap, preaching bone-deep dislike of authority—provided them with a continuing soundtrack to their antisocial behavior. So completely was rap ingrained in their consciousness that every so often, one or another of them would break into cocky, expletive-laden rap lyrics, accompanied by the angular, bellicose gestures typical of rap performance. A couple of his buddies would then join him. Rap was a running decoration in their conversation.

Many writers and thinkers see a kind of informed political engagement, even a revolutionary potential, in rap and hip-hop. They couldn't be more wrong.

Many writers and thinkers see a kind of informed political engagement, even a revolutionary potential, in rap and hip-hop. They couldn't be more wrong. By reinforcing the stereotypes that long hindered blacks, and by teaching young blacks that a thuggish adversarial stance is the properly "authentic" response to a presumptively racist society, rap retards black success.

The Black Criminal Rebel as a Hero

The venom that suffuses rap had little place in black popular culture—indeed, in black attitudes—before the 1960s. The hip-hop ethos can trace its genealogy to the emergence in that decade of a black ideology that equated black strength and authentic black identity with a militantly adversarial stance toward American society. In the angry new mood, captured by [civil rights leader] Malcolm X's upraised fist, many blacks (and many more white liberals) began to view black crime and violence as perfectly natural, even appropriate, responses to the supposed dehumanization and poverty inflicted by a racist society. Briefly, this militant spirit, embodied above all in the Black Panthers, infused black popular culture, from the plays of LeRoi Jones to "blaxploitation" movies, like Melvin Van Peebles's *Sweet Sweetback's Baadasssss Song*, which celebrated the black criminal rebel as a hero.

But blaxploitation and similar genres burned out fast. The memory of whites blatantly stereotyping blacks was too recent for the typecasting in something like *Sweet Sweetback's Baadasssss Song* not to offend many blacks. Observed black historian Lerone Bennett: "There is a certain grim white humor in the fact that the black marches and demonstrations of the 1960s reached artistic fulfillment" with "provocative and ultimately insidious reincarnations of all the Sapphires and Studds of yesteryear."

Early rap mostly steered clear of the Sapphires and Studds, beginning not as a growl from below but as happy party music. The first big rap hit, the Sugar Hill Gang's 1978 "Rapper's Delight," featured a catchy bass groove that drove the music forward, as the jolly rapper celebrated himself as a ladies' man and a great dancer. Soon, kids across America were rapping along with the nonsense chorus:

I said a hip, hop, the hippie, the hippie,
to the hip-hip hop, ah you don't stop
the rock it to the bang bang boogie, say
up jump the boogie,
to the rhythm of the boogie, the beat.

A string of ebullient raps ensued in the months ahead. At the time, I assumed it was a harmless craze, certain to run out of steam soon.

But rap took a dark turn in the early 1980s, as this "bubble gum" music gave way to a "gangsta" style that picked up where blaxploitation left off. Now top rappers began to write edgy lyrics celebrating street warfare or drugs and promiscuity. Grandmaster Flash's ominous 1982 hit, "The Message," with its chorus, "It's like a jungle sometimes, it makes me wonder how I keep from going under," marked the change in sensibility. It depicted ghetto life as profoundly desolate:

You grow in the ghetto, living second rate
And your eyes will sing a song of deep hate.
The places you play and where you stay
Looks like one great big alley way.
You'll admire all the numberbook takers,
Thugs, pimps and pushers, and the big money makers.

Music critics fell over themselves to praise "The Message," treating it as the poetry of the streets—as the elite media has characterized hip-hop ever since. The song's grim fatalism struck a chord; twice, I've heard blacks in audiences for talks on race cite the chorus to underscore a point about black victimhood. So did the warning it carried: "Don't push me, 'cause I'm close to the edge," menacingly raps Melle Mel. The ultimate message of "The Message"—that ghetto life is so hopeless that an explosion of violence is both justified and imminent—would become a hip-hop mantra in the years ahead.

The angry, oppositional stance that "The Message" reintroduced into black popular culture transformed rap from a fad into a multi-billion-dollar industry that sold more than 80 million records in the U.S. in 2002—nearly 13 percent of all recordings sold. To rap producers like Russell Simmons, earlier black pop was just sissy music. He despised the "soft, unaggressive music (and non-threatening images)" of artists like Michael Jackson or Luther Vandross. "So the first chance I got," he says, "I did exactly, the opposite."

Unending Violence and Criminality

In the two decades since "The Message," hip-hop performers have churned out countless rap numbers that celebrate a ghetto life of unending violence and criminality. Schooly D's "PSK What Does It Mean?" is a case in point:

> Copped my pistols, jumped into the ride.
>
> Got at the bar, copped some flack,
>
> Copped some cheeba-cheeba, it wasn't wack.
>
> Got to the place, and who did I see?
>
> A sucka-ass nigga tryin to sound like me.

Put my pistol up against his
head—
I said, "Sucka-ass nigga, I should
shoot you dead."

The protagonist of a rhyme by KRS-One (a hip-hop star who would later speak out against rap violence) actually pulls the trigger:

Knew a drug dealer by the name of
Peter—
Had to buck him down with my 9
millimeter.

Police forces became marauding invaders in the gangsta-rap imagination. The late West Coast rapper Tupac Shakur expressed the attitude:

Ya gotta know how to shake the
snakes, nigga,
'Cause the police love to break a
nigga,
Send him upstate 'cause they
straight up hate the nigga.

Shakur's anti-police tirade seems tame, however, compared with Ice-T's infamous "Cop Killer":

I got my black shirt on.
I got my black gloves on.
I got my ski mask on.
This shit's been too long.
I got my 12-gauge sawed-off.
I got my headlights turned off.
I'm 'bout to bust some shots off.
I'm 'bout to dust some cops off.
. . .
I'm 'bout to kill me somethin'
A pig stopped me for nuthin'!
Cop killer, better you than me.

Cop killer, f--- police brutality! . . .
Die, die, die pig, die!
F--- the police! . . .
F--- the police yeah!

Rap also began to offer some of the most icily misogynistic music human history has ever known. Here's Schooly D again:

Tell you now, brother, this ain't no
joke,
She got me to the crib, she laid me
on the bed,
I f---ed her from my toes to the
top of my head.
I finally realized the girl was a
whore,
Gave her ten dollars, she asked me
for some more.

Jay-Z's "Is That Yo Bitch?" mines similar themes:

I don't love 'em, I f--- 'em.
I don't chase 'em, I duck 'em.
I replace 'em with another one. . . .

Or, as N.W.A. (an abbreviation of "Niggaz with Attitude") tersely sums up the hip-hop worldview: "Life ain't nothin' but bitches and money."

Keeping the Thug Front and Center

Rap's musical accompaniment mirrors the brutality of rap lyrics in its harshness and repetition. Simmons fashions his recordings in contempt for euphony. "What we used for melody was implied melody, and what we used for music was sounds—beats, scratches, stuff played backward, nothing pretty or sweet." The success of hip-hop has resulted in an ironic reversal. In the seventies, screaming hard rock was in fashion among young whites, while sweet, sinuous funk and soul ruled the black airwaves—a difference I was proud of. But in the eighties, rock quieted down, and black music became the assault on the ears and soul. Anyone who grew up in urban America during the eighties won't soon forget the young men strolling down streets, blaring this sonic weapon from their boom boxes, with defiant glares daring anyone to ask them to turn it down.

Hip-hop exploded into popular consciousness at the same time as the music video, and rappers were soon all over MTV, reinforcing in images the ugly world portrayed in rap lyrics. Video after video features rap stars flashing jewelry, driving souped-up cars, sporting weapons, angrily gesticulating at the camera, and cavorting with interchangeable, mindlessly gyrating, scantily clad women.

The occasional dutiful songs in which a rapper urges men to take responsibility for their kids or laments senseless violence are mere garnish.

Of course, not all hip-hop is belligerent or profane—entire CDs of gang-bangin', police-baiting, woman-bashing invective would get old fast to most listeners. But it's the nastiest rap that sells best, and the nastiest cuts that make a career. As I write, the top ten best-selling hip-hop recordings are 50 Cent (currently with the second-best-selling record in the nation among all musical genres), Bone Crusher, Lil' Kim, Fabolous, Lil' Jon and the East Side Boyz, Cam'ron Presents the Diplomats, Busta Rhymes, Scarface, Mobb Deep, and Eminem. Every one of these groups or performers personifies willful, staged opposition to society—Lil' Jon and crew even regale us with a song called "Don't Give a F---"—and every one celebrates the ghetto as "where it's at." Thus, the occasional dutiful songs in which a rapper urges men to take responsibility for their kids or laments senseless violence are mere garnish.

Keeping the thug front and center has become the quickest and most likely way to become a star.

No hip-hop luminary has worked harder than Sean "P. Diddy" Combs, the wildly successful rapper, producer, fashion mogul, and CEO [chief executive officer] of Bad Boy Records, to cultivate a gangsta image—so much so that he's blurred the line between playing the bad boy and really being one. Combs may have grown up middle-class in Mount Vernon, New York, and even [may] have attended Howard University for a while, but he's proven he can gang-bang with the worst. Cops charged Combs with possession of a deadly weapon in 1995. In 1999, he faced charges for assaulting a rival record executive. Most notoriously, police charged him that year with firing a gun at a nightclub in response to an insult, injuring three bystanders, and with fleeing the scene with his entourage (including then-pal Jennifer "J. Lo" Lopez). Combs got off, but his young rapper protegé Jamal "Shyne" Barrow went to prison for firing the gun.

Combs and his crew are far from alone among rappers in keeping up the connection between "rap and rap sheet," as critic Kelefa Sanneh artfully puts it. Several prominent rappers, including superstar Tupac Shakur, have gone down in hails of bullets—with other rappers often suspected in the killings. Death Row Records producer Marion "Suge" Knight just finished a five-year prison sentence for assault and federal weapons violations. Current rage 50 Cent flaunts his bullet scars in photos; cops recently arrested him for hiding assault weapons in his car. Of the top ten hip-hop sellers mentioned above, five have had scrapes with the law. In 2000, at least five different fights broke out at the Source Hiphop Awards—intended to be the rap industry's Grammys. The final brawl, involving up to 100 people in the audience and spilling over onto the stage, shut the ceremony down—right after a video tribute to slain rappers. Small wonder a popular rap website goes by the name rapsheet.com.

Many fans, rappers, producers, and intellectuals defend hip-hop's violence, both real and imagined, and its misogyny as a revolutionary cry of frustration from disempowered youth. For Simmons, gangsta raps "teach listeners something about the lives of the people who create them and remind them that these people exist." 50 Cent recently told *Vibe* magazine, "Mainstream America can look at me and say, 'That's the mentality of a young man from the 'hood.'" University of Pennsylvania black studies professor Michael Eric Dyson has written a book-length paean to Shakur, praising him for "challenging narrow artistic visions of black identity" and for "artistically exploring the attractions and limits of black moral and social subcultures"—just one of countless fawning treatises on rap published in recent years. The National Council of Teachers of English, recommending the use of hip-hop lyrics in urban public school classrooms (as already happens in schools in Oakland, Los Angeles, and other cities), enthuses that "hip-hop can be used as a bridge linking the seemingly vast span between the streets and the world of academics."

How helpful is rap's sexism in a community plagued by rampant illegitimacy and an excruciatingly low marriage rate?

But we're sorely lacking in imagination if in 2003—long after the civil rights revolution proved a success, at a time of vaulting opportunity for African Americans, when blacks find themselves at the top reaches of society and politics—we think that it signals progress when black kids rattle off violent, sexist, nihilistic, lyrics, like Russians reciting [Alexander] Pushkin [who pioneered the use of everyday language in his poems and plays]. Some defended blaxploitation pictures as revolutionary, too, but the passage of time has exposed the silliness of such a contention. "The message of *Sweetback* is that if you can get it together and stand up to the Man, you can win,"

Van Peebles once told an interviewer. But win what? All Sweetback did, from what we see in the movie, was avoid jail—and it would be nice to have more useful counsel on overcoming than "kicking the Man's ass." Claims about rap's political potential will look equally gestural in the future. How is it progressive to describe life as nothing but "bitches and money"? Or to tell impressionable black kids, who'd find every door open to them if they just worked hard and learned, that blowing a rival's head off is "real"? How helpful is rap's sexism in a community plagued by rampant illegitimacy and an excruciatingly low marriage rate?

The idea that rap is an authentic cry against oppression is all the sillier when you recall that black Americans had lots more to be frustrated about in the past but never produced or enjoyed music as nihilistic as 50 Cent or N.W.A. On the contrary, black popular music was almost always affirmative and hopeful. Nor do we discover music of such violence in places of great misery like Ethiopia or the Congo—unless it's imported American hip-hop.

Hardly Progressive

Given the hip-hop world's reflexive alienation, it's no surprise that its explicit political efforts, such as they are, are hardly progressive. Simmons has founded the "Hip-Hop Summit Action Network"[HSAN] to bring rap stars and fans together in order to forge a "bridge between hip-hop and politics." But HSAN's policy positions are mostly tired bromides. Sticking with the long-discredited idea that urban schools fail because of inadequate funding from the stingy, racist white Establishment, for example, HSAN joined forces with the teachers' union to protest New York mayor [Michael] Bloomberg's proposed education budget for its supposed lack of generosity. HSAN has also stuck it to President [George W.]Bush for invading Iraq. And it has vociferously protested the affixing of advisory labels on rap CDs that warn parents about the obscene language inside. Fighting for rappers' rights to obscenity: that's some kind of revolution!

Okay, maybe rap isn't progressive in any meaningful sense, some observers will admit; but isn't it just a bunch of kids blowing off steam and so nothing to worry about? I think that response is too easy. With music videos, DVD players, Walkmans [portable music players], the internet, clothes, and magazines all making hip-hop an accompaniment to a person's entire existence, we need to take it more seriously. In fact, I would argue that it is seriously harmful to the black community.

The rise of nihilistic rap has mirrored the breakdown of community norms among inner-city youth over the last couple of decades. It was just as gangsta rap hit its stride that neighborhood elders began really to notice that they'd lost control of young black men, who were frequently drifting into lives of gang violence and drug dealing. Well into the seventies, the ghetto was a shabby part of town, where, despite unemployment and rising illegitimacy, a healthy number of people were doing their best to "keep their heads above water," as the theme song of the old black sitcom *Good Times* put it.

By the eighties, the ghetto had become a ruleless war zone, where black people were their own worst enemies. It would be silly, of course, to blame hip-hop for this sad downward spiral, but by glamorizing life in the "war zone," it has made it harder for many of the kids stuck there to extricate themselves. Seeing a privileged star like Sean Combs behave like a street thug tells those kids that there's nothing more authentic than ghetto pathology, even when you've got wealth beyond imagining.

The attitude and style expressed in the hip-hop "identity" keeps blacks down. Almost all hip-hop, gangsta or not, is delivered with a cocky, confrontational cadence that is fast becoming—as attested to by the rowdies at KFC—a common speech style among young black males. Similarly, the arm-slinging, hand-hurling gestures of rap performers have made their way into many young blacks' casual gesticulations, becoming integral to their self-expression. The problem with such speech and mannerisms is that they make potential employers wary of young black men and can impede a young black's ability to interact comfortably with co-workers and customers. The black community has gone through too much to sacrifice upward mobility to the passing kick of an adversarial hip-hop "identity."

On a deeper level, there is something truly unsettling and tragic about the fact that blacks have become the main agents in disseminating debilitating—dare I say racist—images of themselves. Rap guru Russell Simmons claims that "the coolest stuff about American culture—be it language, dress, or attitude—comes from the underclass. Always has and always will." Yet back in the bad old days, blacks often complained—with some justification—that the media too often depicted blacks simply as uncivilized. Today, even as television and films depict blacks at all levels of success, hip-hop sends the message that blacks are . . . uncivilized. I find it striking that the cry-racism crowd doesn't condemn it.

For those who insist that even the invisible structures of society reinforce racism, the burden of proof should rest with them to explain just why hip-hop's bloody and sexist lyrics and videos and the criminal behavior of many rappers *wouldn't* have a powerfully negative effect upon whites' conception of black people.

Sadly, some black leaders just don't seem to care what lesson rap conveys. Consider Savannah's black high schools, which hosted the local rapper Camoflauge as a guest speaker several times before his murder earlier this year. Here's a representative lyric:

> Gimme tha keys to tha car, I'm
> ready for war.

When we ride on these niggas
smoke that ass like a 'gar.
Hit your block with a Glock, clear
the set with a Tech. . . .
You think I'm jokin, see if you
laughing when the pistol be
smokin—
Leave you head split wide open
And you bones get broken. . . .

More than a few of the Concerned Black People inviting this "artist" to speak to the impressionable youth of Savannah [Georgia] would presumably be the first to cry out about "how whites portray blacks in the media."

Rap's Present-Day Blaxploitation

Far from decrying the stereotypes rampant in rap's present-day blaxploitation, many hip-hop defenders pull the "whitey-does-it-too" trick. They point to the *Godfather* movies or *The Sopranos* as proof that violence and vulgarity are widespread in American popular culture, so that singling out hip-hop for condemnation is simply bigotry. Yet such a defense is pitifully weak. No one really looks for a way of life to emulate or a political project to adopt in *The Sopranos*. But for many of its advocates, hip-hop, with its fantasies of revolution and community and politics, is more than entertainment. It forms a bedrock of young black identity.

Hip-hop creates nothing.

Nor will it do to argue that hip-hop isn't "black" music, since most of its buyers are white, or because the "hip-hop revolution" is nominally open to people of all colors. That whites buy more hip-hop recordings than blacks do is hardly surprising, given that whites vastly outnumber blacks nationwide. More to the point, anyone who claims that rap isn't black music will need to reconcile that claim with the widespread wariness among blacks of white rappers like Eminem, accused of "stealing our music and giving it back to us."

At 2 AM on the New York subway not long ago, I saw another scene—more dispiriting than my KFC encounter with the rowdy rapping teens—that captures the essence of rap's destructiveness. A young black man entered the car and began to rap loudly—profanely, arrogantly—with the usual wild gestures. This went on for five irritating minutes. When no one paid attention, he moved on to another car, all the while spouting his doggerel. This was what this young black man presented as his message to the world—his oratory, if you will.

Anyone who sees such behavior as a path to a better future—anyone, like Professor [Michael Eric] Dyson, who insists that hip-hop is an urgent "critique of a society that produces the need for the thug persona"—should step back and ask himself just where, exactly, the civil rights–era blacks might have gone wrong in lacking a hip-hop revolution. They created the world of equality, striving, and success I live and thrive in.

Hip-hop creates nothing.

7

Hip-Hop and Rap Lyrics Are Unfairly Criticized for Violence

Edward Rhymes

Edward Rhymes is an academic in sociology, with an emphasis on African American and United States history.

The violent, misogynistic, drug-celebrating, and sexualized lyrics of rap and hip-hop music are unjustly scrutinized because they are held to a racial double standard. The same level of violence, misogyny, exploitation, and indecency is found in the popular music, films, and television series created by white Americans, but they are largely left noncriticized and even sometimes hailed for their so-called artistic value. In actuality, the objectionable elements of rap and hip-hop reflect popular culture as a whole, which glamorizes violence and is characterized by promiscuity and sexism. Furthermore, censoring rap and hip-hop lyrics and removing such albums from record store shelves does not eliminate the pervasiveness of violence and explicit sexuality found in white-controlled mainstream entertainment.

In this composition I will not be addressing the whole of hip-hop and rap, but rather hardcore and gangsta rap. It is my assertion that the mainstream media and political pundits—right and left—have painted rap and hip-hop with a very broad brush. Let me be perfectly clear, hardcore and

Edward Rhymes, "Caucasian Please! America's True Double Standard for Misogyny and Racism," *Black Agenda Report*, August 15–21, 2007. Reproduced by permission. www.blackagendareport.com/index.php?option=com_content&task=view&id=181&Itemid=33.

gangsta rap is not listened to, watched, consumed or supported in my home and never has. I will not be an apologist for anything that chooses to frame the dialogue about Black women (and women in general) and Black life in morally bankrupt language and reprehensible symbols.

Hardcore rap is treated as if it occurred in some kind of cultural vacuum; untouched, unbowed and uninformed by the larger, broader, dominant American culture.

In the wake of MSNBC's and CBS's firing of [radio and television talk show host] Don Imus [who in 2007 called members of the Rutgers University women's basketball team "nappy-headed hos"], the debate over misogyny, sexism and racism has now taken flight—or submerged, depending on your point of view. There are many, mostly white, people who believe that Imus was a fall guy and he is receiving blame and criticism for what many rap artists do continually in the lyrics and videos: debase and degrade Black women. A Black guest on an MSNBC news program even went as far as to say, "Where would a 66-year-old white guy even had heard the phrase '*nappy-headed ho*'"—alluding to hip-hop music's perceived powerful influence upon American culture and life (and apparently over the radio legend as well)—and by so doing gave a veneer of truth to the theory that rap music is the main culprit to be blamed for this contemporary brand of chauvinism. However, I concur with bell hooks, the noted sociologist and black-feminist activist who said that "to see gangsta rap as a reflection of dominant values in our culture rather than as an aberrant 'pathological' standpoint, does not mean that a rigorous feminist critique of the sexist and misogyny expressed in this music is not needed. Without a doubt black males, young and old, must be held politically accountable for their sexism. Yet this critique must always be contextualized or we risk making it appear that the behavior this thinking supports and condones—rape, male violence against women, etc.—is a black male thing. And this is what is happening. Young black males are forced to take the 'heat' for encouraging, via their music, the hatred of and violence against women that is a central core of patriarchy."

A Product of Society

There are those in the media, mostly white males (but also some black pundits as well), who now want the Black community to take a look at hip-hop music and correct the diabolical "double-standard" that dwells therein. Before a real conversation can be had, we have to blow-up the myths, expose the lies and cast a powerful and discerning light on the "real" double-standards and duplicity. Kim Deterline and Art Jones in their essay, *Fear of a Rap Planet*, point out that "the issue with media coverage of rap is not whether African Americans engaged in a campaign against what they see as violent, sexist or racist imagery in rap should be heard—they should. . . . why are community voices fighting racism and sexism in mainstream news media, films and advertisements not treated similarly? The answer may be found in white-owned corporate media's historical role as facilitator of racial scapegoating. Perhaps before advocating censorship of a music form with origins in a voiceless community, mainstream media pundits should look at the violence perpetuated by their own racism and sexism."

Just as the mainstream media and the dominant culture-at-large treat all things "Black" in America as the "other" or as some sort of science experiment in a test tube in an isolated and controlled environment, so hardcore rap is treated as if it occurred in some kind of cultural vacuum; untouched, unbowed and uninformed by the larger, broader, dominant American culture. The conversation is always framed in the form of this question: "What is rap's influence on American society and culture?" Never do we ask, "What has been society"s role in shaping and influencing hip-hop?"

Gangsta and hardcore rap is the product of a society that has historically objectified and demeaned women, and commercialized sex. These dynamics are present in hip-hop to the extent that they are present in society. The rapper who grew up in the inner-city watched the same sexist television programs, commercials and movies; had access to the same pornographic and misogynistic magazines and materials; and read the same textbooks that limited the presence and excluded the achievements of women (and people of color as well), as the All-American, Ivy-league bound, white kid in suburban America. It is not sexism and misogyny that the dominant culture is opposed to (history and commercialism has proven that). The dominant culture's opposition lies with hip-hop's cultural variation of the made-in-the-USA misogynistic themes and with the Black voices communicating the message. The debate and the dialogue *must* be understood in this context.

If the brutality and violence in gangsta rap was truly the real issue, then shouldn't a series like The Sopranos *be held to the same standard?*

Popular Culture's Duplicitous Sexism and Violence

In a piece I penned a couple of years ago, I endeavored to point out the clear ethnic and racial double-standards of the media and society as it pertains to sex and violence. My assertion was, and remains to be, that the mainstream media and society-at-large, appear to have not so much of a problem with the glorification of sex and violence, but rather with *who* is doing the glorifying. In it I stated that "if the brutality and violence in gangsta rap was truly the real issue, then shouldn't a series like *The Sopranos* be held to the same standard? If we are so concerned about bloodshed, then how did movies like *The Godfather*, *The Untouchables* and *Goodfellas* become classics?"

I then addressed the sexual aspect of this double-standard by pointing out that *Sex and the City*, a series that focused, by and large, on the sexual relationships of four white women, was hailed as a powerful demonstration of female camaraderie and empowerment. This show, during its run, was lavished with critical praise and commercial success while hip-hop and rap artists are attacked by the morality police for their depiction of sex in their lyrics and videos. The don't-blink-or-you'll-miss-it appearance of Janet Jackson's right bosom during [a] Super Bowl halftime show . . . caused more of a furor than the countless commercials that (also aired during the Super Bowl) used sex to sell anything from beer to cars to gum. Not to mention the constant stream of commercials that rather openly talks about erectile dysfunction medication.

The exaltation of drugs, misogyny and violence in music lyrics has a history that predates NWA, Ice Cube, Ice-T and Snoop Dogg.

The exaltation of drugs, misogyny and violence in music lyrics has a history that predates NWA [Niggaz with Attitude], Ice Cube, Ice-T and Snoop Dogg. Elton John's 1977 song "Tickin'" was about a young man who goes into a bar and kills 14 people; Bruce Springsteen's "Nebraska," featured a couple on a shooting spree, and his "Johnny 99," was about a gun-waving laid-off worker; and Stephen Sondheim's score for "Assassins," which presented songs mostly in the first person about would-be and successful presidential assassins.

Eric Clapton's "Cocaine" and the Beatles' "Lucy in the Sky with Diamonds" (LSD) as well as almost anything by Jefferson Airplane or Starship. Several songs from *Tommy* and Pink Floyd's *The Wall* are well-known drug songs. "Catholic girls,"

"Centerfold," "Sugar Walls" by Van Halen were raunchy, misogynistic, lust-driven rock refrains. Even the country music legend Kenny Rogers in his legendary ballad, "Coward Of The County," spoke of a violent gang-rape and then a triple-homicide by the song's hero to avenge his assaulted lover. Marilyn Manson declared that one of the aims of his provocative persona was to see how much it would take to get the moralists as mad at white artists as they got about 2LiveCrew. He said it took fake boobs, Satanism, simulated sex on stage, death and angst along with semi-explicit lyrics, to get the same screaming the 2LiveCrew got for one song. Manson thought this reaction was hypocritical and hilarious.

Other artists like Kid Rock have won commercial success easily and faced only minor battles with the FCC [Federal Communications Commission] with songs such as: "F--- U Blind." Consider the lyrics of Kid Rock, whose piercing blend of hard rock, metal and misogyny has sold millions of records:

Now if you like the booty come on
fellas show it
This is your last verse to wax so
why would you blow it
And if the ladies if you are tired of
a man on your fanny
Then f--- you go home and watch
the tube with granny . . .
Just look at all the girls that are
dying to get some
Man, just don't be a wussy
And I'll guarantee you could get a
piece of p----

Likewise, consider the lyrics of the rock song "Anything Goes" from Guns N Roses:

Panties 'round your knees
With your ass in debris

Doin' dat grind with a push and squeeze
Tied up, tied down, up against the wall
Be my rubbermade baby
An' we can do it all.

The bad-boy, outlaw rockers have traditionally and consistently been marketed and packaged as misogynistic. Artists and groups such as David Lee Roth, Kid Rock, Metallica, Uncle Kracker, to name a few. Take note of the following list of rock groups and some of the albums and songs that they have released: American Dog (released an album in 2001 titled, *Six Pack: Songs About Drinkin & F---in*), Big C-ck (released an album in 2005 titled: *Year Of The C-ck*—with titles like "*Bad Motherf---er*", "*Hard To Swallow*" & "*You Suck the Love Out of Me*"), W.A.S.P. (released an album in 1983 titled: *Animal: F--ks Like A Beast*, an album in 1997 *K.F.D.: Kill, F---, Die*), Faster Pussycat (released album in 1992 titled *Whipped*—with a song titled "*Loose Booty*," 2001 titled: *Between the Valley of the Ultra P--sy*, 2006 album titled: *The Power of The Glory Hole*—with such titles as "*Porn Star*" and "*Shut Up & F---*"), Lynch Mob (released an album in 2003 titled: *Evil: Live*—featuring the song ("*Tie Your Mother Down*") and a compilation album released in 2003 titled *C-ck N' Roll: The World's Sleaziest Rock Bands*—displaying "hits" like: Dog Sh-t Boys—"*One Minute F---*," Sagger—"*The Closest I've Ever Come To F---ing Myself*" and Hellside Stranglers—"*Motherf---ers Don't Cry*.")

The Focus on Black Artists

In an article by Dana Williams titled, "Beyond Rap: Musical Misogyny," Ann Savage, associate professor of telecommunications at Butler University stated: "It's the repetitiveness of the messages, the repetitiveness of the attitudes, and it builds on people. . . ." "People say rap is dangerous. Yes, rap music does have misogyny, but there has always been an objectification and misogyny against women in music," said Savage. "Yet we focus on the black artists, not the rockers and not even the white executives who are making the big money from this kind of music."

Savage further asserts that the race-based double standard applies to violent content in music as well. "There was the Eric Clapton remake of [reggae artist Bob] Marley's 'I Shot the Sheriff,' and there was little to be said. But then you have the 'Cop Killer' song by Ice-T and it's dangerous and threatening."

In this same article Cynthia Fuchs, an associate professor at George Mason University, affirmed that "the public seems far more disturbed by misogynistic lyrics in the music of rap and hip hop artists who are largely black than similar lyrics in rock music, perceived by most as a white genre."

"The flamboyance of rock is understood as performance, rather than from the perspective of personal feelings," said Fuchs, who teaches courses in film and media studies, African American studies and cultural studies. "These guys are seen as innocuous. They appear to be players in the fence of accumulating women in skimpy costumes, but they aren't necessarily seen as violent. The mainstream takes it (hip hop and rap) to represent real-life, so it's seen as more threatening than some of the angry, whiney white boy rock, even though the same messages and images are portrayed."

Moreover, in a piece titled "C-ck Rock" from the October 21–November 3, 2003, edition of the online music magazine *Perfect Pitch*, it was revealed that when the *Hustler* founder and entrepreneur Larry Flynt wanted to combine the worlds of porn (the ultimate god of misogyny) and music he did not turn to rap, but rather to rock. It was stated that since porn has been mainstreamed, they wanted a more "contemporary" look—and when they looked for a contemporary look, did they seek out the likes of Nelly, Chingy, 50 Cent or Ludacris? No. Rock legend Nikki Sixx was chosen to "grace" the cover of *Hustler*'s new venture along with his adult-entertainment and former *Baywatch* star girlfriend Donna D'Errico wearing nothing but a thong and Sixx's arms.

"To the white dominated mass media, the controversy over gangsta rap makes great spectacle."

The Double-standard Applied to Rap Music

It is my belief that this paradigm; this unjust paradox, exists because of the media stereotypes of black men as more violence-prone, and media's disproportionate focus on black crime (which is confused with the personas that rappers adopt), contribute to the biased treatment of rap. The double standard applied to rap music makes it easier to sell the idea that "gangsta rap" is "more" misogynist, racist, violent and dangerous than any other genre of music. However, I believe that bell hooks conceptualized it best in her essay "Sexism and Misogyny: Who Takes the Rap?": "To the white dominated mass media, the controversy over gangsta rap makes great spectacle. Besides the exploitation of these issues to attract audiences, a central motivation for highlighting gangsta rap continues to be the sensationalist drama of demonizing black youth culture in general and the contributions of young black men in particular. It is a contemporary remake of *Birth of a Nation* [the 1915 silent film featuring white supremacist themes] only this time we are encouraged to believe it is not just vulnerable white womanhood that risks destruction by black hands but everyone."

Part of the allure of gangsta or hardcore rap to the young person is its (however deplorable) explicitness. The gangsta rapper says "bitches" and "hos," defiantly and frankly (once again . . . deplorable) and that frankness strikes a chord. However, it is not the first time that a young man or woman has seen society "treat" women like "bitches" and "hos." Like mother's milk, the American male in this country has been "nourished" on a constant diet of subtle messages and notions regarding female submission and inferiority and when he is weaned, he begins to feed on the meat of more exploitative mantras and images of American misogyny long before he ever pops in his first rap album into his CD player. Young people, for better or worse, are looking for and craving authenticity. Now, because this quality is in such rare-supply in today's society, they gravitate towards those who appear to be "real" and "true to the game." Tragically, they appreciate the explicitness without detesting or critically deconstructing *what* the person is being explicit about.

There have been many who have said that even with Imus gone from the airwaves, the American public in general and the Black community in particular will still be inundated by the countless rap lyrics using derogatory and sexist language, as well as the endless videos displaying women in various stages of undress—and this is true.

However, by that same logic, if we were to rid the record stores, the clubs and the iPods of all misogynistic hip-hop, we would still have amongst us the corporately-controlled and predominantly white-owned entities of *Playboy*, *Penthouse*, *Hustler* and *Hooters*. We would still have the reality TV shows, whose casts are overwhelmingly white, reveling in excessive intoxication and suspect sexual mores. If misogynistic hip-hop was erased from American life and memory today, tomorrow my e-mail box and the e-mail boxes of millions of others would still be barraged with links to tens of thousands of adult entertainment web sites. We would still have at our fingertips, courtesy of cable and satellite television, porn-on-demand. We would still be awash in a society and culture that rewards promiscuity and sexual explicitness with fame, fortune and celebrity (reference Anna Nicole [Smith], Paris Hilton, Britney Spears).

And most hypocritically, if we were to purge the sexist and lewd lyrics from hip-hop, there would still be a multitude of primarily white bands and principally white musical genres generating song after song glorifying sexism, misogyny, violence and lionizing male sexuality and sexual conquest.

8

Hip-Hop and Rap Lyrics Offer Positive Messages

Sara Libby

Sara Libby is an editor for Creators Syndicate, which distributes syndicated columns and comic strips.

Critics who contend that the lyrics of hip-hop and rap are violent and misogynistic frequently fail to see the positive messages many of the songs deliver. Though some lyrics are suitable only for adult audiences, the hits of many hip-hop and rap artists and groups—from hip-hop pioneers Salt-N-Pepa to current chart toppers like Ludacris—convey themes of empowerment and the importance of education and nonviolence, as well as affirming images of women. Also, hip-hop and rap serve as a gateway for youths to other forms of expression, such as poetry and dance.

In the aftermath of the [television and radio host] Don Imus debacle [in which Imus called the Rutgers University women' basketball team "nappy-headed hos", everyone from conservative pundits to rap mogul Russell Simmons has pointed a finger at hip-hop, arguing that while Mr. Imus's rant was inappropriate, rap stars get away with such sexist and racially charged language on a daily basis. And sure, there are plenty of rap songs that celebrate homophobia, intolerance, and women-bashing. But to say that hip-hop comprises only those qualities is like saying that country artists croon solely about pickup trucks.

Sara Libby, "Hip-hop's Bad Rap," *Christian Science Monitor*, May 3, 2007. Reproduced by permission of the author. www.csmonitor.com/2007/0503/p09s01-coop.htm.

I grew up in virtually all-white McMinnville, Ore., and, save for the occasional minority scholarship I didn't qualify for, have never been discriminated against. Yet, thanks to the magic of MTV, I became transfixed by hip-hop at an early age—begging my mom for rides to the local record store to pick up releases by LL Cool J, Dr. Dre, and the Beastie Boys. In each album, I found something familiar and relatable. In the gangstas trying to escape the violence of Compton, Calif., I saw myself wanting out of a small, stifling farm town; their rants against the police reminded me of teachers and others who never took the time to understand my perspective.

The fact that I—a petite, well-educated blond woman—am rushing to defend rap music should at least make you think twice before condemning hip-hop as a genre that celebrates violence and sexism.

Never once did listening to rap make me run out and buy a gun or sleep around. Rather, I was empowered by Salt-N-Pepa telling me "fight for your rights, stand up and be heard/ you're just as good as any man, believe that, word" and impressed by Tupac Shakur's willingness to rap unabashedly about his love for his mama.

When I moved to Los Angeles for college, I joined other young intellectuals in classes on black pop culture and black literature, where I was often the only white student. I was inspired to study the lynching of [African American teenager] Emmett Till after hearing him mentioned not by Bob Dylan [a white singer and songwriter], but in a song by rapper Kanye West.

A Critical Difference

Which is why I've been dumbfounded by critics who have recently characterized rap as strictly the domain of materialists and misogynists. Honestly, has Bill O'Reilly [the conservative commentator] ever actually sat down and listened to a single rap song in its entirety? (Disclosure: I work for the company that syndicates his column.) The pundit's favorite whipping boy has been the rapper Ludacris, whom he lambastes for using profanity and referencing violence. But the last time I checked, Ludacris's recent hit was "Runaway Love," in which he spotlights domestic violence against women with concern and care.

When I go on my daily afternoon run, the first song on my workout mix is "I Can" by Nas, in which he addresses young blacks, telling them: "Nobody says you have to be gangstas, hos/ read more, learn more, change the globe." And just this morning, I heard a radio commercial by rapper Nick Cannon, who also hosts a hip-hop-themed show on MTV, imploring young people to check out community college as a way to better themselves.

[Hip-hop is] a medium that pleads for its audience to take part in their communities—and one that increasingly affirms women as teachers and role models.

Another one of the past year's best-selling rap artists, T.I., seduces a woman on the song "Why You Wanna" not by saying he wants to slap her behind, but by offering to "compliment you on your intellect and treat you wit respect." Yes, the lyrics are punctuated by R-rated language and imagery, but there's a critical difference between a song's profanity and its underlying message.

Some would argue—perhaps rightly so—that using terms such as "ho" and the "N" word is never OK, no matter what the context. But rap, like all music, is simply a reflection of the society that gave rise to it—and America's in particular is one with a centuries-old history of relegating blacks and women to the bottom of the barrel, something white men were practicing long before the Sugar Hill Gang and other early rap groups came along.

If hip-hop detractors really cared about the generation they insist is being corrupted, they should also acknowledge the surprising amount of good that hip-hop does as a vehicle that opens young people's eyes to poetry and dance. It's a medium that pleads for its audience to take part in their communities—and one that increasingly affirms women as teachers and role models.

9

Banning Words from Hip-Hop and Rap Music Would Be Beneficial

John H. McWhorter

John H. McWhorter is a senior fellow at the Manhattan Institute, a political and economic research organization. He is the author of several books, including Winning the Race: Beyond the Crisis in Black America, Doing Our Own Thing: The Degradation of Language, *and* Music in America and Why We Should, Like, Care.

Hip-hop record label owner Russell Simmons's call for a voluntary ban on the words "bitch," "ho," and the N-word is a milestone for the entertainment industry and African American culture. Numerous intellectuals and chart-topping hip-hop and rap artists have long contended that their usage—particularly the N-word—is part of "keeping it real." However, rationalizing African Americans' use of such words in music lyrics and everyday speech is an apathetic response to racism and sexism. As a prominent figure in hip-hop and rap, Simmons's denouncement of this abusive language sets a precedent for the African American community to follow and is a momentous shift toward equality.

Just as we could thank George III [of England] for creating the United States of America, black America can now thank [television and radio host] Don Imus [who referred to members of the Rutgers University basketball team as "nappy-headed hos"] for making Russell Simmons finally face himself. On Monday Mr. Simmons, co-founder of Def Jam Records, called for a voluntary ban on the N-word, "bitch" and "ho'" in rap music, and suggested that the words be bleeped when music with them is broadcast. Meanwhile, the NAACPA [National Association for the Advancement of Colored People] has spearheaded a STOP campaign aimed at combating the use of these words and the imagery associated with them, in popular culture.

This is a moment for the history books.

There is a consensus that there is something really wrong with black people using these words with such glee, meanwhile supporting the billion-dollar industry that wallows in it.

In fact, there has been an ongoing "conversation" in the black community and beyond, about black people's use of the N-word among themselves, and in rap music. It's been a staple topic in the media, in call-in radio shows and on panels for several years. But at times it has been hard to glean much purpose in this conversation.

On the one hand there is a consensus that there is something really wrong with black people using these words with such glee, meanwhile supporting the billion-dollar recording industry that wallows in it. Yet after the speeches, history lessons and chin-scratching are over, the N-word, "bitch" and "ho'" continue to reign supreme, lexical staffs of life in top-selling rap.

"Keeping it Real"

What's the justification? Well, we are told that the very wondrousness of this music is that it is "keeping it real." It has been especially depressing to watch "hip-hop intellectuals" pontificating on this theme. Hearing rap denounced as sexist, for example, they tartly remind us that there is sexism in American society as a whole—suddenly blind to the obvious issue of degree. And this from people who brandish a tripwire sensitivity to the minutest gradations of racism.

This worship of the "real" has done black America no favors, beyond making some entertainers and producers very rich. The civil rights heroes of the past were devoted to getting America past the racism and segregation that were once quite "real." It used to be considered a hallmark of human societies that their members strive beyond the "real"—creating legal codes, religions and even art.

The idea that black people ought now sit back and savor the "reality" of abusive language, including the same word that the Bull Connors [a Ku Klux Klan member and segregation advocate] of the world once hurled at us in all of its "reality," is in essence lazy. It is an incoherent rationalization by people who are merely intoxicated by the rhythms and politically inclined to thrill to black voices from the street.

Looking Inward

Two weeks ago [in April 2007] there was little reason to expect a return to basic standards of decency and dignity among the folks so besotted with the fascinations of the "real." Mr. Simmons and [civil rights activist] Benjamin Chavis issued a manifesto in the wake of the Imus controversy, insisting that this kind of language in hip-hop was "reality" not to be "censored."

One assumed that the language on these recordings would only change very gradually, as the result of a change in black America's self image, the increasing hybridization of the population, or perhaps just fashion. Every once in a great while, however, one witnesses a phase shift, when events conspire to force an abrupt and significant change in the cultural landscape.

It would appear that something about the Imus episode really struck a chord in a way that earlier events did not. [Former Republican senator] George Allen's macaca comment [directed at a volunteer of his opponent's campaign who is of Indian descent] was rather obscure; [former "Seinfeld" star] Michael Richards's gaffe [in which he shouted racist remarks, including the N-word, at African American hecklers during a comedy routine] was a peculiar, nervous outburst from a washed-up comedian. But Mr. Imus had influence and a long record of verbal tackiness; the fact that he was referring to young, talented women rendered his comment stingingly mean. The usual routine—screaming bloody murder, while nevertheless insisting that black men using the same words on bestselling CDs is "real"—suddenly felt inconsistent, not to mention small and even uncomfortably close to self-loathing.

Most debates on race boil down to the question as to whether black America's main problem is racism or culture—that is, whether [comedian] Bill Cosby is right [in his comments attacking African American slang and speech patterns]. Over the past several years, it has become increasingly mainstream among blacks to understand that questioning aspects of black culture is a matter not of ignorance or ill will, but of survival. There is a growing perception that even if all racism were somehow removed as of this Friday, black Americans would still have a lot of work to do.

How truly awesome it is that this week [in April 2007], one of the hip-hop industry's creators and a civil rights organization (so addicted to chasing "racism" that a new president committed to social services instead didn't even last two years) have committed themselves to the black community looking inward.

We cannot hope to control private conversation—as a quick listen to the way so many black, Latino and even many Asian teens now talk to one another will so easily demonstrate. However, we can have more control over the public sphere—if only its powers that be get in line. Mr. Simmons and the NAACP just did.

10

Banning Words from Hip-Hop and Rap Music Would Not Be Beneficial

Alexander Billet

Alexander Billet is a music journalist and activist living in Washington, DC. He is working on his first book, The Kids Are Shouting Loud: The Music and Politics of the Clash.

Hip-hop record label owner Russell Simmons's call for a voluntary ban on the three controversial words from hip-hop and rap—"bitch," "ho," and the N-word—is an unsatisfactory and unfair solution to eliminating sexism and racism. Banning these words limits the voices of African American artists who comment on racial oppression and poverty in the United States and does not address the misogyny prevalent in "white" music. Furthermore, Simmons's high stakes in the recording industry, as well as his current political and corporate ties, place into question his motivations. Ultimately, the focus on "sexist" and "racist" hip-hop and rap lyrics undermines the discussions about racial and gender equality that they are meant to provoke.

It's hard to know what to think about Russell Simmons's recent announcement about checking the content of hip-hop. There is no denying that most of us would like the words "bitch," "ho," and "nigger" to disappear from the English lexicon entirely. But alas, the situation is much more complicated than that. On the one hand, it is true that sexism and ho-

Alexander Billet, "Is Russell Simmons Playing Politics with Hip-Hop?" *ZNet Commentary*, May 8, 2007. Reproduced by permission of the author. www.zmag.org/Sustainers/Content/2007-05/08billet.cfm.

mophobia abound in not just rap but popular culture as a whole. On the other, there is a need to defend the music against those who denounce it for political gain.

And on yet a third hand (or maybe a foot), we have the context of the announcement in midst of a backlash against the glorious sacking of [television and radio host] Don Imus [who called the Rutgers University women's basketball team "nappy-headed hos"].

Apples and Oranges

To be clear, Imus' supposed defense that he was merely repeating the "language" in hip-hop is the biggest pile of crap since? well, his show. Hip-hop is a response to the long-term degradation of blacks and other oppressed peoples in the United States. Like all music it is flawed, but like no other genre it remains a mirror held up to the worst ills in American society. Imus, on the other hand, is a mouthpiece for maintaining those ills. A well-paid veteran broadcaster, he has spent the past twenty-plus years calling Arabs "rag-heads," gay men "faggots," and black women "cleaning ladies." He brought his producer on board because he liked "nigger jokes." And all the while he has interviewed the most high-profile politicians, media moguls and millionaires on his show. Imus and hip-hop are in completely different leagues.

Furthermore, to say that sexism is somehow unique to rap is laughable. Listen to anything by Merle Haggard or Ted Nugent, the Rolling Stones' "Cat Scratch Fever," [actually, a Nugent song] or the hit from Fountains of Wayne "Stacy's Mom" (whose video featured a stereotypical "MILF" [a physically attractive mom] parading around in stripper gear) and one might get a good idea of how rife so-called "white" music is with misogyny.

But the twisted logic of this defense seems to have soaked well past Imus himself. [Illinois senator and presidential candidate] Barack Obama (whose own role in assuaging white liberal guilt becomes bigger and bigger every day) made it clear which side he stood on with his comments last week [in May 2007]: "We've got to admit to ourselves that it was not the first time that we heard the word 'ho.' Turn on the radio station. There are a whole lot of songs that use the same language and we've been permitting it in our homes, in our schools, and on iPods." So, Barack, how long until you revive the PMRC [Parents Music Resource Center, a committee formed in 1985 that called for record companies to place parental advisory labels on recordings containing offensive language or content]?

It is the same kind of bootstrap rhetoric we've been hearing from Obama since day one. It's the kind of talk that bolsters the idea that racism doesn't exist, and blacks are only poor because they're lazy and self-loathing. When Obama spends more time talking about "getting Uncle Jethro off the couch" [a comment Obama made in a speech believed to allude to encouraging reticent black Americans to become active in the voting process] than he does about Hurricane Katrina, any criticism he may have of hip-hop should be put on mute.

Muddying the Message

Enter Russell Simmons. At times, his own defense of hip-hop has been eloquent and prescient. His response to Obama [in his comments regarding Don Imus] provided a glimpse into the nature of this debate: "People who are angry and come from tremendous struggle; they have poetic license, and when they say things that offend you, you have to talk about the conditions that create those kinds of lyrics. When you are talking about a privileged man who has a mainstream vehicle and mainstream support and is on a radio station like that you have to deal with them differently."

Yet less than a week later, Simmons and his Hip-hop Summit Action Network announces it is launching a campaign to better the content of Simmons' own Def Jam recordings. In particular, he wants to crack down on the use of the words "ho," "bitch," and "nigger." Though a dialogue about such a thing is welcome, it should be initiated by the artists themselves, not by a label owner. When it is initiated by someone in Simmons's position, and at a time such as this, one wonders if this "discussion" is happening because of a genuine need, or rather because of pressure from the same people who are threatened by hip-hop's very existence.

First of all, neither Obama, Oprah [Winfrey], or any of the more right-wing figures diverting the issue seem to know anything about hip-hop. One wonders why there is no mention of the socially hard-hitting rhymes of the Roots, Common or Talib Kweli. Or even some of the more conscious (if still contradictory) mainstream joints coming from the likes of Nas or Kanye West.

Perhaps it's because there are those who have made billions off marketing rap's worst elements, while downplaying its long history of being a forum to speak out on inequality and poverty. Ever since Grandmaster Flash's "The Message" first hit the airwaves, the likes of MTV, BET and Clear Channel have sought ever more effective methods of making rap marketable by dumbing it down. That's called exploitation.

Hip-hop historian Jeff Chang illustrated such marketing patterns with the example of Nas' *Stillmatic* in a 2002 article. Though the album was full of protests against war and racism in the post-9/11 world, it also included songs with homophobic language chronicling his beef with Jay-Z. Needless to say, the latter got the airplay, but the former was ignored.

It's All About the Cheddar

Given this, it is questionable how much Simmons himself will actually be able to change. He may have direct control over the content that his own label puts out, but Def Jam is still subject to the same market principles as any other major record label. With Clear Channel having a strangle-hold on radio airplay, and likewise with MTV on television, will Simmons's efforts make a difference?

An MC friend of mine from Baltimore recently pointed out that Simmons lives in a very different world than most of the acts on his label. Despite his admirable record on civil rights issues, Simmons's more recent behavior may indicate somewhat of a shift. Many progressive hip-hop fans were dismayed when he endorsed Maryland's Republican Lieutenant Governor Michael Steele for Senate last election. When he received criticism for organizing a tour through Africa with DeBeers Jewelers, Simmons responded that there is too much focus on conflict diamonds [diamonds mined in African war zones that are sold in secret to fund the conflicts].

Might his endorsement of Steele be just the beginning? Might this announcement be more than a publicity stunt, but a concession to Obama and the likes? Is it possible that beneath his progressive image, Simmons is attempting to buddy up to this country's heavy-hitting politicos?

Simmons's action opens the door for those who want to do away with not just the "sexist" or "misogynistic" elements, but hip-hop altogether.

Only time will tell, but there is a bigger problem. In making this announcement about hip-hop's content now, in the context of a backlash in response the Imus firing, Simmons' concession seems to say that the two are linked. They aren't. Worse still, Simmons's action opens the door for those who want to do away with not just the "sexist" or "misogynistic" elements, but hip-hop altogether. John McWhorter of the conservative Manhattan Institute has stated he makes no distinction between "conscious" rap and "gangsta" rap. He sees both as violent and depraved. When it comes down to it he would also probably like to squash the art form altogether. Simmons has now opened the door to McWhorter's arguments.

The Imus scandal should be an opportunity to talk about the very real racial and gender inequality in this country. It should be the chance to ask why women make 75 cents to men's dollar. To ask why more black men are in prison than college, and why the NYPD [New York Police Department] thought it necessary to pump fifty rounds into [African American police violence victim] Sean Bell's car. Instead, the debate has shifted to all the flaws in black culture, and has merely reinforced the double standard that "white" culture simply isn't held up to. Where will Russell Simmons take the debate? Only time will tell, but it doesn't look promising.

11

Advisory Labels and Recording Industry Self-Regulation Are Effective

Hilary Rosen

Hilary Rosen is chairwoman and chief executive officer of the Recording Industry Association of America, a trade organization that represents over six hundred record companies.

The recording industry effectively regulates the marketing and distribution of music with explicit or mature content. The Parental Advisory program requires that these albums and singles, as well as related advertisements and other promotional materials, prominently display Parental Advisory labels. In addition, unlike the rest of the entertainment industry, recording companies release edited versions of albums and singles originally containing explicit or mature content that are appropriate for young audiences and mainstream airplay. Thus, the recording industry successfully maintains its responsibility to parents while respecting the freedom of expression of recording artists and the choices of consumers.

I am Hilary Rosen, Chairman and CEO [chief executive officer] of the Recording Industry Association of America [RIAA], an association that represents over 600 record companies.

I welcome this opportunity to provide you with the details of our industry's efforts since this Subcommittee's review last July [2001].

Hilary Rosen, "Prepared Witness Testimony, Recording Industry Marketing Practices: A Check-Up, Subcommittee on Telecommunications and the Internet," October 1, 2002. http://energycommerce.house.gov/reparchives/107/hearings/10012002Hearing718/Rosen1197.htm.

There are two points that I would like to raise at the outset: (1) the unwavering commitment of our industry to the success of the Parental Advisory Program; and (2) my concern that the recording industry's "marketing practices" have not been evaluated by the FTC [Federal Trade Commission] in a manner that fairly takes into account the specific nature of music and mass advertising that includes no more than one demographic group at the same time.

The recording industry takes its responsibility seriously.

First, I would like to underscore that the recording industry takes its responsibility to parents and consumers very seriously. The Parental Advisory has been in existence for seventeen years [since 1985]. We created this program, have guided its development, and are proud of its impact. Moreover, we value the respect and trust that we have developed with parents over the years.

I have met personally with each of the major record companies to review the implementation of our guidelines and we have been meeting with our retail partners as well. There is a commitment at every level in the recording industry to the continued success of the Parental Advisory Program.

We produce and market a diverse range of sounds.

The recording industry releases over 36,000 albums each year. The vast majority of these titles contain no explicit content. In fact, I would like to note that despite the emphasis at these hearings on recordings with explicit content, they comprise a relatively small proportion of our industry's output. In an average retail store with 110,000 titles, about 500 will carry the Parental Advisory logo. That's less than one-half of one percent of that store's total inventory. Moreover, the overwhelming majority—if not all—of the titles that are explicit are also available in an edited version. Unlike any other entertainment industry, music lovers have a choice. If a movie is rated "R", a consumer does not have the choice to see a "PG" version in the theatre or to purchase it in the store. When considering advertising of an album, the availability of an edited version should be taken into account. The industry is not advertising an explicit album, it is advertising an album available in two versions.

Parents overwhelmingly recognize and support the Parental Advisory Program.

Let me now turn to the significant steps we have taken over the last year to ensure the continued success of the Parental Advisory Program.

The industry continues to strengthen its guidelines.

An important aspect of our commitment to the Program is making sure that it evolves to meet the changing needs of retailers and parents without compromising the twin principles that guide it: (1) alerting parents to explicit content; and (2) protecting the First Amendment rights of artists to free expression.

We recently implemented changes to the guidelines that accomplish this goal. The RIAA has published revised guidelines that became effective on April 1, 2002. The guidelines include three new provisions:

- The implementation of an "Edited Version" Label on packaging: If an edited version of an album designated with the Parental Advisory Label [PAL] is released, it should include an "Edited Version" Label plainly displayed either on the front of the album (on the cellophane wrapper or on the album cover itself), or on the top spine of the CD. The Edited Version Label is a notice to consumers that an album has been modified from the original, and does not include all of the same content contained in the Labeled version.
- Adoption of an "Edited Version Also Available" Label in advertising: If an "edited" version of a recording is

available for sale, consumer print advertising may contain language indicating that fact. This will be accomplished with the wording "Edited Version Also Available" placed near the specific album or sound recording that has been designated with the Label.

- The extension of the existing guidelines for print advertising to radio and television promotions: In cases where the decision has been made to place a Parental Advisory Label on a recording, all consumer print, radio, and television advertising (collectively "consumer advertising") for that recording shall communicate the presence of explicit content.

The Recording Industry Is Adhering to its Guidelines

In February 2001, the FTC issued a report on the industry's implementation of its guidelines and gave us a failing grade. I came before this Committee and indicated that we deserved that failing grade. I also stated that future reviews would demonstrate progress. We have kept our word and have made significant progress.

- All of the major record companies have issued internal policy guidelines and have appointed a senior level employee to ensure full compliance with the Parental Advisory Program, including the new provisions.
- According to the Commission's February 2001 study: only 8% of print ads in reviewed magazines displayed the PAL. According to our review of the October and November issues of the same magazines reviewed by the FTC that number is now nearly 100 percent. In fact, there was only one ad that did not carry the Logo, and the album in that add is available in an edited version.

- 100 percent of the PAL's were clearly legible.
- Additionally, parental controls have been included on many online subscription services with an "exclude explicit content" option check box: "Check here if you would like to exclude tracks from albums that contain a Parental Advisory logo. A description of the Parental Advisory Program can be found at http://www.parentalguide.org."

We have continued our educational outreach efforts.

Parents overwhelmingly recognize and support the Parental Advisory Program. All of the recent surveys on this issue have confirmed that fact. We have not, however, rested on our laurels. We continue our efforts to raise public awareness about the Parental Advisory Program.

- The RIAA designed and distributes an informational brochure in English and Spanish for parents and caregivers describing:

  The evolution of the Parental Advisory Label,

  How determinations for its application are made,

  And the meaning of the label with suggestions for links to community-service based organizations.

- The RIAA and its members have worked to ensure "Edited Version Also Available" has been quickly integrated into the consumer lexicon.
- The RIAA have worked on creative methods of distributing the PAL PSA [public service announcement], including in video magazines.
- The RIAA continues to partner with the National Association of Recording Merchandisers (NARM) on many fronts, including updating all parental advisory label displays in retail stores.

- Additionally, we have established a partnership with the Association for Independent Music (AFIM) to further advance our educational outreach efforts.

I am proud of the significant strides we have made in the last year. We are committed to continuing to work hard to ensure the Parental Advisory Program remains successful and a priority for our industry.

Informational rating systems should reflect the nature of their respective industries.

Our labeling system is often compared to the ratings systems in place for the television, motion picture and videogame industries. While our industries work together to bring information about our systems to parents through the www.parentalguide.org website, our systems are very different. And for good reason. Each system is designed and has evolved to reflect the media to which it applies.

Advertising an album available in two versions to a mixed audience is far different than targeting kids with explicit material.

We think that it would be unwise and improper to assume that a record label knows what kind of music and lyrical content is "suitable" for whom. Like books or poetry, different listeners will take away different meanings from musical recordings and their lyrics, making a "one-size-fits-all" determination particularly unsuitable. Record labels should not be in the business of making assumptions about the values or maturity levels of their customers. The purpose of the advisory label is to provide a clear "heads-up" to all consumers that a sound recording contains explicit content. Books have no label or rating, even those that contain explicit content and are marketed directly to children. Why? Because words are particularly subject to interpretation and imagination, and most feel that labeling books is a bad idea. Lyrics likewise are susceptible to varying interpretations. Words can have different meanings depending on who is hearing them. We offer alternatives and trust that consumers will [make] the choice that is best for them.

Moreover, advertising an album in a publication where a significant percentage of those who see it are over 17 years of age should not be regarded as intentionally "targeting children." Advertising an album available in two versions to a mixed audience is far different than targeting kids with explicit material. Yet it is described in such a manner for purposes of government review.

No Regulation Is Necessary

In summary, the recording industry has in place a system that works—one that reflects the nature of the art form; is being strengthened and promoted; and is overwhelming[ly] supported by America's parents.

To its credit the Federal Trade Commission has recognized that the First Amendment precludes government intervention in this area and that "vigilant self-regulation is the best approach to ensuring that parents are provided with adequate information to guide their children's exposure to entertainment media with violent content."

We have proven over the last year that self-regulation is the way to progress. In the last year, we have seen at the state level that efforts to regulate content are fraught with danger. Some states have even imposed criminal penalties for failing to adhere to voluntary standards. Rather than improving parents' access to information, such statutes create a disincentive to adopting voluntary standards. By essentially punishing those who adopt voluntary guidelines, the legislation would have the unintentional result of discouraging participation in the successful Parental Advisory Program. Fortunately, these statutes have been challenged in the Courts and ruled unconstitutional.

Without regulation we have strengthened our guidelines and have seen tremendous improvement in the areas explored by the FTC. Without regulation, one of our members has expanded on our voluntary program and now provides content descriptors. This experiment by BMG will give us some insight into whether content descriptors will work with music and whether consumers will find it helpful or confusing.

What is clear from the debate on the state and national level is that at bottom there are some people who simply don't like some types of music. That is fine. You have the option of listening to and purchasing what you do like. What we don't have the option of doing is silencing some voices based on personal prejudices. Taking away angry music will not take away angry feelings. Society and life is more complicated than that. We are willing to do our part by providing parents and consumers generally with information and choices in the music. They must also accept their role in the process.

In the end, I am proud that the RIAA's Parental Advisory Program and the balance we have struck in respecting the free expression of artists while providing information and choice to consumers.

Thank you.

12

Advisory Labels and Recording Industry Self-Regulation May Not Be Effective

Mike Osegueda

Parental Advisory labels, which warn consumers that albums or singles have objectionable content, may have lost their effectiveness because popular music has dramatically changed. Despite the recording industry's measures, popular music is becoming increasingly explicit, making these labels commonplace. In fact, young consumers, who were once drawn to the shock value of the labels, have become indifferent to them altogether. Furthermore, the battle for decency in popular music has been replaced by the crusade against illegal music downloading and file-sharing. Though some parents may find Parental Advisory labels preferable to having no labeling system in place, it merely reaffirms to consumers that rock and rap music are the sounds of rebellion.

The year was 1985.

Popular music and society were two trains on a collision course. Parents of a teen who killed himself sued rocker Ozzy Osbourne, saying his song "Suicide Solution" aided their son.

Wal-Mart stopped selling rock 'n' roll magazines such as *Spin*, *Rolling Stone* and *Tiger Beat*.

Mike Osegueda, "Warning Fable," *Fresno Bee*, February 13, 2005.

Tipper Gore, the wife of Sen. Al Gore, and Susan Baker, the wife of Secretary of State James Baker, rallied a group of powerful political wives calling themselves the Parents Music Resource Center, protesting violent and sexual content in music.

As the often-told story goes, it all began with Gore hearing her daughter Karenna, then 11, singing along to Prince's song "Darling Nikki"—specifically a lyric about masturbating in a hotel lobby.

When the parents group released its "Filthy Fifteen," the targets of its crusade on crude music, Prince topped the list, along with AC/DC, Black Sabbath, Cyndi Lauper, Def Leppard, Judas Priest, Madonna, the Mary Jane Girls, Mercyful Fate, Mötley Crüe, Sheena Easton, Twisted Sister, Vanity, Venom and W.A.S.P.

That's when popular music's train crashed right into society's train. The collision was big and explosive, with carnage everywhere.

Swooping in for damage control was the Record Industry Association of America, which, in November of 1985, agreed to a labeling system that would be placed on music products to warn parents about violent, sexual or other questionable content.

It was then that the well-known, black-and-white "Parental Advisory—Explicit Lyrics" sticker was born.

Our Music Culture Is Different Today

Now it's 2005. Twenty years later, some things have changed. Others haven't.

Ozzy Osbourne is as famous for being a television parent as a rocker. Madonna's a mother changing filthy diapers. Prince is a Jehovah's Witness. But Wal-Mart still won't sell explicit CDs.

And has anybody heard from Mercyful Fate, Sheena Easton, Twisted Sister, Vanity, Venom or W.A.S.P. lately, let alone questioned their musical content?

Gore and Baker's group has all but vanished. The fight to keep music clean is still going on to some degree, but downloading has overtaken explicit content as the objection du jour in the music world.

The "Parental Advisory" label, meanwhile, has become so common that it's ingrained in our culture, much like the "Do Not Remove" tag on a pillow.

The "Parental Advisory" label, meanwhile, has become so common that it's ingrained in our culture, much like the "Do Not Remove" tag on a pillow. It's something we see, acknowledge, sometimes joke about—but do people still pay attention to it?

And more importantly, 20 years later, has it made a difference? Are the two trains still on a collision course? Or have they set off in opposite directions?

Our music culture is different today. We have digital music, burned CDs and music videos—all of which have become animals of their own.

Before, it was all about a black-and-white sticker no bigger than an adult thumb. Back then, could Tipper Gore and Susan Baker have even fathomed how their little sticker would fare in the digital music era?

It was 1990 by the time the "Parental Advisory" label started being universally applied. After 1985, different forms of the label were used, but none universally until the record industry's label was unveiled in 1989 and applied in 1990.

In the years between Gore's outrage and the sticker, the controversy grew behind the rise of gangster rap (starting with N.W.A. [Niggaz with Attitude]) and the notoriously sexified 2 Live Crew.

Once the stickers were in place, things were complicated even further. Retailers were refusing to sell certain albums. Employees at music stores were getting fined and arrested for selling to children albums marked explicit—most notably 2 Live Crew's "Nasty As They Want to Be." Have you heard about that lately?

Exactly.

Plain and Ordinary

The sticker itself has moved away from the spotlight. While it was once the center of attention, having a sexy reputation that caused kids to seek out albums containing it, today the label has settled into its place: sitting in the corner, looking plain and ordinary.

A study by the Federal Trade Commission in July 2004 said that 83% of teenagers were able to walk into a store and buy a CD with a "Parental Advisory" sticker without problem. That number is down from 90% in 2001 and about even with 85% in 2000.

"The use of the Parental Advisory sticker both on packaging and in advertising has increased over time," trade commission attorney Dick Kelly says. "So it's more often used than it was at the start of our project. Video games and movies are, in general, doing more in the way of disclosing rating information, but at the same time, there has been improvement."

This means the warning label has become more visible in advertisements for music products, which includes noting that edited versions of explicit albums are available.

"The program works well," said Jonathan Lamy, a Recording Industry Association of America spokesman, in a statement. "We've found that parents are satisfied with the program and believe it to be effective. The Parental Advisory label is visually recognizable to parents and has remained consistent in appearance for 20 years."

The Federal Trade Commission and others have called for a more detailed, more specific rating system, similar to that of the video game, television and movie industries.

"The purpose of the program is to provide a heads-up to all consumers that a sound recording contains explicit content," the record industry's statement said. "Unlike age-based ratings systems, a label is applied to all recordings containing explicit content. We think it would be unwise and improper to assume that a record label, or the government for that matter, knows what kind of musical and lyrical content is suitable for whom."

The closest thing to an expanded warning label came from BMG [music company] in 2002, it detailed explicit content in a way similar to television and movie ratings. Its use, however, is intermittent.

Other, smaller changes have happened with little effect.

The "Parental Advisory" logo changed from stickers to labels printed directly on CD covers and the wording was changed from "Explicit Lyrics" to "Explicit Content."

A new fight has come with trying to implement "Parental Advisory" tactics with digital music. Most legal pay-to-download sites now feature online warning labels.

A False Sense of Security

However, illegal file-sharing and copying of CDs leave parents unprotected if they're trying to keep tabs on what their kids are listening to, which the industry—steadfast in its anti-illegal-file-sharing stance—is quick to point out.

Of course, if you listen to the doubters of the program, that doesn't matter anyway.

"It hasn't worked by anyone's measure," says Eric Nuzum, a free-speech advocate and author of *Parental Advisory*, a book about music censorship. "If parents use that sticker as a measure for what their kids should and shouldn't buy, they are luring themselves into a false sense of security. It's more used as [a] defensive measure than a tool for parents."

On their lunch break at [California's] Fresno High on Thursday [in February 2005] a huddle of teenagers agreed that "Parental Advisory" labels don't dictate at all what music they buy.

"Nobody cares about it," says Jeff Legler, 17. "And parents don't check. My mom's a conservative Christian, and she doesn't even care. She doesn't even know what it is."

"It's been out there so long," says Sarah Reyes, 17, "that people are used to seeing it."

So here we are. It's 2005. Twenty years later. A day and age when you can turn on the radio in the middle of the day and hear 50 Cent saying, "Shake that ass, girl."

In 1997, Juvenile had a major hit, "Back That Azz Up," that was changed to "Back That Thang Up" for the radio.

Is this a sign of filthy music seeping further into our kids' minds? Or are society's standards getting lower?

Rock and rap music were both born out of rebellion—as a way for adolescents to separate themselves from adults. A "Parental Advisory" label isn't going to stop that.

"It's worse," says Tim Wildmon, president of the American Family Association. "From the videos and the lyrics, the pop stars like Britney Spears and Christina Aguilera and some of the hip-hop artists, they're singing a lot about sex. It's unfortunate that that message is going out to 11-, 12-, 13-, 14-year-old kids. You can put labels on the CDs, which is helpful. It's not the end-all, be-all, but it's helpful. It gives parents some notification who don't have any clue who the groups or singers are."

But it's worth noting that, at one point, Elvis Presley was once threatened with arrest on obscenity charges if he moved his hips.

"I don't really notice a change over the last 15 years," says E. Curtis Johnson, the director of programming for Clear Channel Radio in Fresno and a 29-year veteran of the industry. "Some of that is perspective. What one person notices isn't necessarily what another person does. From my perspective, there's always been a rather liberal stance from the recording community about what's accepted and what isn't. The things that I found objectionable in 1985 are still things that I've found objectionable in 2005."

Rock and rap music were both born out of rebellion—as a way for adolescents to separate themselves from adults. A "Parental Advisory" label isn't going to stop that. If anything, it'll help.

"Is music going to continue to get more and more explicit?" Nuzum says. "Popular music only needs to be one step further along. If you want to know what popular music is going to be like, look at the television news every night. Look at the rhetoric on talk shows. Look at the newspaper. If all of the sudden it's shocking to hear 'ass' on the radio, look at the political discourse in this country and see how that has changed."

Organizations to Contact

The editors have compiled the following list of organizations concerned with the issues debated in this book. The descriptions are derived from materials provided by the organizations. All have publications or information available for interested readers. The list was compiled on the date of publication of the present volume; the information provided here may change. Be aware that many organizations take several weeks or longer to respond to inquiries, so allow as much time as possible.

American Decency Association
PO Box 202, Fremont, MI 49412
(231) 924-4050 • fax: (231) 924-1966
e-mail: info@americandecency.org
Web site: www.americandecency.org

The American Decency Association strives to educate its members and the general public on matters of decency and to initiate, promote, encourage, and coordinate activity designed to safeguard and advance public morality consistent with biblical Christianity.

American Family Association (AFA)
PO Drawer 2440, Tupelo, MS 38803
(662) 844-5036 • fax: (662) 842-7798
Web site: www.afa.net

Founded in 1977, AFA represents and stands for traditional family values, focusing primarily on the influence of television and other media on society. Though it does not support censorship, AFA advocates responsibility and accountability of the entertainment industry. The association believes that through its various products, the entertainment industry has played a major role in the decline of those values on which our country was founded and which keep a society and its families strong and healthy. AFA publishes a monthly newsletter and *AFA Journal*.

Freemuse
Nytorv 17, Copenhagen K DK-1450
Denmark
+45 33 32 10 27
e-mail: freemuse@freemuse.org
Web site: www.freemuse.org

Freemuse is an independent international organization advocating freedom of expression for musicians and composers worldwide. It is membership based, with its secretariat based in Copenhagen, Denmark, and was formed at the first World Conference on Music and Censorship held in Copenhagen in November 1998.

Hip-Hop Association (H2A)
PO Box 1181, New York, NY 10035
(212) 500-5970 • fax (212) 300-4895
e-mail: info@hiphopassociation.org
Web site: www.hiphopassociation.org

H2A is a nonprofit organization with national headquarters in Harlem, New York. Its goal is to use hip-hop culture as a tool to facilitate critical thinking and foster social change and unity by empowering communities through the use of media, technology, education, and leadership development while preserving hip-hop culture for future generations.

National Association for the Advancement of Colored People (NAACP)
4805 Mt. Hope Dr., Baltimore, MD 21215
(877) NAACP-98 (622-2798)
Web site: www.naacp.org

NAACP is a civil rights organization that works to ensure the political, educational, social, and economic equality of rights of all persons and to eliminate racial hatred and racial discrimination. It formed the STOP Campaign to combat demeaning images of African Americans in the media, particularly African American women, and conducted a mock funeral for the N-word in July 2007.

National Coalition Against Censorship (NCAC)
275 Seventh Ave., New York, NY 10001
(212) 807-6222 • fax: (212) 807-6245
e-mail: ncac@ncac.org
Web site: www.ncac.org

NCAC, founded in 1974, is an alliance of fifty national non-profit organizations, including literary, artistic, religious, educational, professional, labor, and civil liberties groups. The coalition works to educate its members and the public at large about the dangers of censorship and how to oppose it.

Recording Industry Association of America (RIAA)
1025 F St. NW, Washington, DC 20004
(202) 775-0101
Web site: www.riaa.org

RIAA is the trade group that represents the U.S. recording industry. Its mission is to foster a business and legal climate that supports and promotes its members' creative and financial vitality. RIAA members create, manufacture, and distribute approximately 90 percent of all legitimate sound recordings produced and sold in the United States.

Bibliography

Books

Peter Blecha	*Taboo Tunes: A History of Banned Bands & Censored Songs*. San Francisco: Backbeat Books, 2004.
Steven Brown and Ulrik Volgsten, eds.	*Music and Manipulation: On the Social Uses and Social Control of Music*. New York: Berghahn Books, 2005.
Martin Cloonan and Reebee Garofalo, eds.	*Policing Pop*. Philadelphia: Temple University Press, 2003.
Steve Jones, ed.	*Pop Music and the Press*. Philadelphia: Temple University Press, 2002.
Marie Korpe, ed.	*Shoot the Singer! Music Censorship Today*. London: Zed Books, 2004.
Allan F. Moore, ed.	*Analyzing Popular Music*. New York: Cambridge University Press, 2003.
Eric Nuzum	*Parental Advisory: Music Censorship in America*. New York: Perennial, 2001.
Roy Shuker	*Popular Music: The Key Concepts, 2nd Ed.* New York: Routledge, 2002.
Chris Washburne and Maiken Derno, eds.	*Bad Music: The Music We Love to Hate*. New York: Routledge, 2004.

S. Craig Watkins — *Hip Hop Matters: Politics, Pop Culture, and the Struggle for the Soul of a Movement*. Boston: Beacon, 2005.

Periodicals

Terry Armour — "Chicks Still Have a Lot to Say About Censorship," *Chicago Tribune*, November 15, 2006.

Associated Press — "Rappers Cleaning Up Post-Imus," August 2, 2007.

Associated Press — "Study Links Degrading, Lewd Music to Teen Sex," August 7, 2006.

Tim Cavanaugh — "Artists for Censorship," *Reason*, April 27, 2004.

Derrick Z. Jackson — "Epithet Stung, Even for Pryor," *Boston Globe*, December 14, 2005.

Steve Knopper — "Sticker Shock 'Parent Warning' Labels Can't Seem to Please Anyone," *Denver Rocky Mountain News*, July 26, 2003.

Colleen Kottke — "C'mon Parents, Face the Music!" *Reporter*, August 29, 2007.

Annie Nakao — "Throwing the Book at Music Censors," *San Francisco Chronicle*, May 30, 2004.

New Internationalist "Sound Facts: While Radical Musicians Often Risk Censorship or Worse in Many Parts of the World, the Global Entertainment Industry Helps Keep Them Poor and Disenfranchised While Reaping Huge Profits," August 2003.

Amanda Paulson "Misogyny—Set to Music—May Alter Teen Behavior," *Christian Science Monitor*, August 8, 2006.

Claude Robinson "Music, Morals, and Money," *Jamaica Observer*, October 10, 2004.

Kelefa Sanneh "Don't Blame Hip-hop," *New York Times*, April 25, 2007.

T. Denean Sharpley-Whiting "Pimpin' Ain't Easy: Hip-hop's Relationship to Young Women Is Complicated, Varied and Helping to Shape a New Black Gender Politics," *Colorlines Magazine*, May–June 2007.

Christopher Thompson "Curbing Homophobia in Reggae," *Time*, August 7, 2007.

Nigel Williamson "Banned! Music Censorship Spans Globe, and U.S. Is No Longer Stranger to Trend," *Billboard*, May 22, 2004.

Index

D

E

F

G

H

M

N

O

P

R

S